***HARRY G. FLINNER*

THE BRIGHT SIDE
OF THE
APOCALYPSE

Harry G. Flinner

****
****

A Study in the Book of Revelation

Published by
APOC Publishing
1465 Pleasant Street
Springfield, Oregon, 97477

Copyright 1995 by Harry G. Flinner
First printing 1995
Printed in the United States of America
Morris Publishing, Kearney, NE

Library of Congress Cataloging in Publication Data 95-94999
Flinner, Harry G.
The Bright Side of the Apocalypse: A new approach to the study of the Book of Revelation. The author has chosen not to follow the confusing traditional theological position but rather chose a popular view that is both logical and understandable.

ISBN 1-57502-055-6 $11.95 Soft Cover

Printed in the USA by

Morris
PUBLISHING

3212 E. Hwy 30
Kearney, NE 68847
800-650-7888

THE BRIGHT SIDE OF THE APOCALYPSE

Preface

For thirty-five years I have been studying the Book of Revelation, and have read nearly every prominent book on the subject. I have taught the Book of Revelation many dozens of times in Seminaries, Bible Schools and Churches. To me this is the most   fascinating of all 66 books of the Holy Scriptures. I read the Revelation of John and rejoice, but when I read what others write explaining what John wrote I am struck with panic and terror. Most are prophets of gloom and doom. Devastation, destruction, judgment, pain, suffering and death seem to be the theme of their writings. I do not see the Book of Revelation in that light. For that reason I have chosen to write on THE BRIGHT SIDE OF THE APOCALYPSE.

2 The Bright Side of the Apocalypse

How can there be a bright side to the apocalypse? Is that not a contradiction of terms? In no way. Webster's dictionary defines the word apocalypse as "a religious writing depicting symbolically the end of evil." This is precisely what the Revelation of John is all about. It is a book of redemption. It is the completion of God's plan of salvation. The message is upbeat and positive. I see the last book of the Bible as the final chapter in God's plan of redemption. It is the story of the Church, the redeemed ones. It is the story of the glorious Church without spot or wrinkle. You and I are a part of that company of the redeemed and we are the principle characters in the unraveling of this exciting drama. There is a bright side of the apocalypse.

A STUDY OF THE BOOK OF REVELATION

Introduction

"In the beginning..." Thus begins our Bible, and so begins the drama of creation. We read these words and look back to a point in history when only God existed. There was not a speck of dust, not a breath of air, not a spark of light, nor a pulse of energy. No one knows how long ago that was. The estimates vary from less than 10,000 years to billions of years ago. It matters not when, but that point "in the beginning" marks the beginning of time from which the age of the universe is measured. When scientists have finally discovered and dated some moon rock or meteorite that was part of that created matter, that date marks the beginning of time.

John goes back to that beginning of time in two other books that he wrote. The first verse of the Gospel of John reads, "In the beginning was the Word and the Word was with God and the Word was God. The same was in the beginning with God." He starts there again in the First Epistle of John with the words, "That which was from the beginning declare we unto you." And here in the Book of Revelation he refers once again to that beginning, quoting the words of the triumphant, glorified Christ, "I am ALPHA and the OMEGA, the beginning and the ending."

Just as certain as time had a beginning it will have an ending. There is coming a day when time shall be no more. Eternity will begin again. In the eternity before creation God existed alone. There was no matter, there was no created life, there was nothing but God. It will never be like that again. A hundred million years from now you and I will exist in a tangible, beautiful world of God's creation.We were created by God in His own image to share His fellowship and companionship. That was the relationship that Adam had with God in the Garden of Eden. God came down in the cool of the day to walk with Adam as His friend.

We are familiar with the story of how sin entered that garden, interrupted that fellowship and broke that relationship.That story begins many years before man was created. Sin did not originate with Adam and Eve in the Garden of Eden. Sin began in the heart of an archangel named Lucifer who was cast out of heaven for his pride and rebellion. It was he, Lucifer, who took the form of a serpent and beguiled our forefather in the garden. It was that sin that plunged the world into chaos and decay. As the result of that sin, what God had created pure and beautiful was made ugly and dirty; what God had created immortal became mortal. "And so sin entered into the world and death passed upon all men." is the way the Apostle Paul put it. It is a sad and disastrous story, but it is not the end. Revelation reveals the ending of that drama of creation.

Just as the Book of Genesis deals with the opening chapters of creation, the fall of man and the early years of the human race; the Book of Revelation deals with the closing chapter of that same drama. Our understanding of the Bible is incomplete without an understanding of the closing chapter. That chapter is the Book of Revelation.

The word "revelation" has a very clear and simple meaning -- a revealing, an unveiling. Yet Martin Luther did not include this book in his translation of the Bible. To him the Book of Revelation was obscure, confusing, symbolic and without interpretation. In his day that was so. In these latter days the Revelation is becoming more and more clear. The truth is that a layman today can have a better understanding of the message of Revelation than did such noted scholars as Luther, Wesley, Knox or Calvin. In the past these great teachers did not understand the meaning of

Revelation and how it pertained to the Rapture and the Second Coming.

The Book of Revelation concerns the unveiling of Jesus Christ. It is the story of His triumphant return to earth to possess and restore this planet as a suitable habitation for His people. Christ has a glorious future prepared for us. This is not a story of doom and gloom. Christian writers and preachers who predict the end of the world and the futility of life are prophets of doomsday. Their message is negative and hopeless. Christian parents have even considered it ill-advised to bring children into this world. "The end is at hand." "There is no hope." "What is the use of planning and building for tomorrow when there won't be any tomorrow?"

No, my friend. That is not the message of God's Word. God has revealed to us the beautiful, marvelous plan He has for this earth and for His people. No dictator, no atheistic nation, no world power, no nuclear war, nor any other satanic force will ever thwart that plan. The world is not coming to an end. We, God's people, are going to inhabit this planet Earth for a long time into the future. We will live on this planet in the most prosperous, happy, productive, meaningful society imaginable.

What God has planned for us is not simply

eternal life. It will not be mere existence. Don't ever believe that heaven consists of our sitting on a cloud playing a harp throughout an endless eternity. We will learn in this study a great deal about what eternity will be like. But the Word assures us that "Eye hath not seen, nor ear heard, neither hath it entered into the heart of man the things that God hath prepared for those who love Him." No matter how beautiful, exciting and glorious a picture I might paint of heaven, we know that the half has never yet, nor ever will be told.

Friend, this is no message of doom and gloom. When Paul wrote, "Look up for your redemption draweth nigh," he was not thinking of doom and disaster. He was looking at a plan and project designed by God for us. The revelation of Jesus Christ is the revealing, the unveiling of that plan. It will be a future full of joy and anticipation, not fear and dread. What God has planned for us is so great and so glorious that Jesus said, "It would be better for you to pluck out your eyes and go through life blind, or cut off an arm and go through life maimed than to miss it."

Let us get into the study of what I feel is the most fascinating book of the Bible. "Blessed is he that readeth and he that heareth the words of this prophecy, and keep those things which are written therein for the time is at hand." Revelation 1:3. No other book of the Bible bears that promise of blessing.

No other book in the Bible is written quite like this one. John, "the beloved" disciple, the fisherman brother of James is the writer of the book. He is not the author, only the writer. This message was authored by God Himself and was delivered to John by an angel. It seems that this angel accompanied John throughout the writing of this book. The Book of Revelation was not inspired in the same way other books of the Bible were inspired. When John was given this message he was literally caught up into heaven, he was projected into the future and was actually seeing and experiencing what was to transpire two thousand years later. What he saw makes a fantastic story. We are going to follow John and that angel through his same incredible odyssey.

I am eager to know who was that angel who met John that Lord's Day on Patmos, escorted him into heaven, accompanied him back to earth and served as his "tour guide" throughout this tremendous unforgettable adventure. It could be that this was the same angel before whom John fell in worship in the final chapter, Revelation 22:8

"And I John saw these things and heard them.

And when I had heard and seen, I fell down to worship before the feet of the angel which showed me these things."

In the next verse the angel is identified as one of John's fellow servants. He was no "angel" at all. In all probability what John thought was an angel was one of the Apostles; but in his spiritual, glorified, transformed body John did not readily recognize him. There will be many times in the Book of Revelation when John sees a transformed human being, or a company of such people in their spiritual bodies, and identifies them as angels. He refers to the pastors of the seven churches as angels. This is only one of the many mysteries we will unravel as we get into the study of this awesome book.

Awesome is probably the right word to describe the Book of Revelation, as you and I sit back in awe while this story unfolds before us. It wasn't an easy story for John to tell. We need to look carefully at the language he uses and the difficulty John had in communicating the message that was given to him.

This is the problem: John wrote this book about 70 years after the death of Christ. The vision he saw was of scenes taking place some 2000 years in the future. How would John describe in the language of a fisherman of the first century the marvels he saw in the 20th century? How would he describe a computer, a satellite, an atomic bomb, a helicopter, a rifle or a truck? How would he describe a thousand other things that are of our generation and were totally foreign to him? He had no way of putting names to them. What if he had? Supposing he had called a helicopter a "washindacu." We would have no idea what he meant by that term. For that reason John did not attempt to give new names to any of the strange things he saw. How he must have marveled at the spectacular scenes that he witnessed as he was catapulted into our century. John had a formidable problem in communicating to us that experience, for it all had to be told in language we would understand 2000 years later.

Once we can understand the language John used we can more easily interpret what he was saying. I am not talking about being able to understand Greek, the language in which John wrote. There are excellent translations of that Greek text into English. The King James Bible is quite adequate for our use. You could read several translations of the Book of Revelation but you will discover that none of them clarify what John is attempting to say. When we read what John said, translated into the King's best English, it is still "Greek" to most of us.

It is not a better translation that we need. We must discover some basic rules of interpretation to be able to understand what John was thinking. Once we grasp these simple concepts and apply them consistently to our study, we will discover to our amazement that the darkest and most difficult passages of this book become clear and understandable.

There are three types of language that John uses in his writing of this book. (1) Symbolic (2) Figurative and (3) Literal.

As for symbolic language, there are very few symbols used in the entire book of Revelation. We use symbols all the time. A flag is a symbol. The skull and crossbones are a symbol. Railroad crossing signs are symbols. Many traffic signs are symbols. Some symbols are easy to understand while others need an explanation. When John uses a symbol in his writings he generally gives an explanation of that symbol.The symbol of the seven golden candlesticks that John saw in Revelation 1:12 are explained in 1:20.

"The seven golden candlesticks are the seven churches."

Whenever John uses symbolic language, a careful study of the context will reveal the meaning. For that reason symbolic language is easy. Figurative language is a bit more difficult to comprehend.

Figurative language is very common in the Bible and in our everyday use. If an unhappy consumer says that his car is a "lemon", his description has nothing to do with citrus fruit. We know exactly what he means. To speak with a "forked tongue" does not describe how the tongue looks. When we say "he sure was a heavy" we are not describing a person's physical weight. When John the Baptist said, "Behold the Lamb of God that taketh away the sins of the world," no one expected to see a four-footed, woolly, bleating sheep. Figurative language does not describe the physical appearance of a person or thing, but rather his or its function. There is something in the character, personality, action or function of the person or thing that is being described. Look at an example. John is describing Jesus Christ in Revelation chapter one in the following terms

".....clothed with a garment down to the foot, and girt about the paps with a golden girdle. His head and His hairs were white like wool, as white as snow; and His eyes were as a flame of fire; And His feet like unto fine brass, as if they burned in a furnace; and His voice as the sound of many waters. And He had in His right

hand seven stars: and out of His mouth went a sharp two-edged sword;   and His countenance was as the sun shineth in his strength."

John is not describing literally what he saw. There is no two-edged sword in Jesus' mouth. His feet are not of burned brass and His voice did not sound like a waterfall. We must interpret the meaning of this language in the light of the character, the personality, the action or the function of Jesus as revealed elsewhere in the entire Bible, but particularly in the Book of Revelation. This is the joy of Bible study. The Holy Spirit can reveal to you the meaning of figurative language as surely as He can reveal it to a great theologian.Many of the obscure passages are not all that obscure if we simply remember that John is probably writing in figurative language.

The third style of writing is the use of literal language. Admittedly, literal language is the most difficult to understand. John chose to use literal language that will carry the true meaning of his message to any age or generation. He does not give new names to countries that did not exist in his day. He chooses to use the ancient or contemporary names. He chooses to use literal language of his day to describe what did not exist in his day. He uses swords, horses and chariots as instruments of war; when in reality he might be describing tanks, missile launchers and trucks of our day. Let me give you an example of what I mean. Two hundred years ago Benjamin Franklin said, "The pen is mightier than the sword." The meaning of that statement is just as true today as it was 200 years ago;   but today for pen we use printing presses, typewriters and word processors; and for the sword weapons of the atomic age. But the message remains the same.

I firmly believe that the message of the Book of Revelation was written to be understood. John was endeavoring to communicate his message. If we understand the types of language that John chose to use we will better be able to comprehend what he was trying to say. Of course we must use common sense in our reading. There are passages in the Book of Revelation that speak of horses, and indeed the horses are horses.   John will speak of ships that, in reality, are ships. It may sound confusing. Nevertheless, when you complete this study you will have a clearer understanding of this mysterious book than you ever thought possible.

Prepare yourself for a totally absorbing experience as we plunge into a study of the Book of Revelation. I don't expect this to be an abstract Bible study about prophecy. You and I will be carried into the future with John the Apostle, share the fantastic scenes that he describes, and participate in the incredible revelation that unfolds before us.

THE BRIGHT SIDE OF THE APOCALYPSE
LESSON ONE

DIVISION ONE

**John's encounter
with Jesus Christ**

Chapter 1

REVELATION CHAPTER ONE

After the brief introduction of verses 1 through 3 John addresses himself to the seven churches who are to be the recipients of this message. Obviously these seven churches are seven congregations of believers located in various cities of Asia Minor. Some of these churches are mentioned in the Book of Acts and others in the Epistles of Paul; while others are not found anywhere else in the Bible. We are going to study these churches in greater detail in chapters two and three. These were not only actual churches of Asia Minor, but they were representative churches of the distinctive church epochs of ecclesiastical history from Ephesus to the Rapture.

One important matter must be clarified before we study the seven churches. Although the three books of the Bible: Revelation, Daniel and Ezekiel are talking about the same time; they do not deal with the same subject matter. The Book of Daniel is prophecy concerning the nations of the earth. The Book of Ezekiel is prophecy concerning the Jews. The Book of Revelation is prophecy concerning the church. The only time the Jewish nation is mentioned in the Book of Revelation is where it deals with the 144,000 chosen from each of the twelve tribes. However, these had all converted to Christianity and were part of the church. Our understanding of this prophecy will be much clearer if we keep in mind that the church is the only theme of the Book of Revelation.Then the writings of Daniel, Ezekiel, Matthew and Paul all shed light on our study rather than add confusion. Historically the Book of Revelation is a continuation of the Book of Acts. Chapter two begins with the Church of Ephesus which was the primitive Church of the early first century the Church of the Book of Acts.

Revelation 1:1-8
Greetings From The Trinity

John was nearly 100 years old when he wrote this book. He was exiled on the isle of

Patmos in the Eastern Mediterranean Sea, and was left there to die. All the other apostles had long since died. Many of their deaths had been violent and horrendous. The apostle John was the only disciple to die a natural death and that occurred not many years after writing the Revelation.

John begins with greetings from three persons in verses four and five of chapter one. The three persons are (1) God the Father "The one which is, which was, and is to come." (2) God the Spirit "The seven Spirits which are before the throne." and (3) God the Son, "Jesus Christ who is the Faithful Witness." We can not make a correct interpretation of the prophecy of the Book of Revelation unless we can identify the three persons of the Trinity as they appear in the unraveling of this drama of the Apocalypse. The story begins in verse nine.

Revelation 1:9-20
Jesus Christ Meets With John

John was alone as far as any human company; yet he was conducting a worship service, practicing the presence of Jesus. He was singing hymns and spiritual songs, quoting Scriptures, praying and worshipping as was his custom on the Lord's Day. It made no difference to him that no one else was there. But suddenly John was aware that someone else was there. He was not alone. "I heard behind me a great voice," he said, "saying, 'I am ALPHA and OMEGA, the beginning and the ending..." John turned around see who was speaking. He had heard that voice 70 years before. but he never had heard it speak with such power and authority. The one he saw was none other than his friend and teacher, his Lord and Master whom he had known intimately for three years, plodding the dusty footpaths of Palestine. The last time he had seen Him was on the Mount of Olives.That was the day the Lord ascended into the heavens and disappeared behind the clouds.

I am sure that John's heart pounded with excitement when he recognized the voice. There was a familiar aspect that John could recognize, and there was also a majestic aspect of His glorified state that left John spellbound and awestruck. You and I will experience that same sensation when we see Jesus face to face. He is so close and intimate with us now, but when we see Him in all of His glory we will all stand back in awe and wonder.

John sensed that wonder. Something special was taking place before his eyes. In a panoramic view   the congregations of seven selected churches passed before him.   He recognized these churches. He knew just where they were located in each town. He was acquainted with each congregation. Probably he personally knew every pastor of those seven churches.

In the figurative language that John chose to use to describe this scene he says that these seven pastors, or angels as he calls them, were held in the right hand of Christ. That is not what he saw. Remember John is not describing what he saw. The pastors were not there at all. They were back home shepherding their congregations. John is describing, not what he sees, but what is happening. Figurative language is the only way that he could express this thought. The figure is beautiful. God is holding us in the palm of His hand. It is the same figure of speech used by Christ in John chapter 10, "No man shall be able to pluck us out of the right hand of God." This is a good example of figurative language. The lesson we learn in this first chapter is that John does not attempt to describe the physical characteristics or appearance of what he sees, but rather he describes something about the personality, actions, or function of the person about whom he writes. Of course, too, as we have already suggested, the seven golden candlesticks and the seven stars are a good example of symbolic language and how that is clarified in the context.

There is little more that needs to be said about chapter one. The text will yield its meaning to any reader of the Word who is looking to the Holy Spirit to enlighten his understanding.

THE BRIGHT SIDE OF THE APOCALYPSE

LESSON II

DIVISION TWO

The Church on Earth
From Pentecost to the
Rapture

Chapters 2 and 3

REVELATION CHAPTER TWO

You will notice in a red letter edition of the Bible that all of chapters two and three are in red letters, indicating that these are the words of Jesus, not of John nor of an angel. Some of the messages are addressed to the pastor (called an angel by John) and others are addressed to the congregation. Each of these brief messages is to a specific church congregation that existed in John's day in the area known today as Asia Minor. Some were prominent churches that were located in cities that exist even today. Others were written to obscure congregations in small and insignificant communities that have never been located by archeologists or historians.

There is a reason why these particular seven church congregations were selected. Each of them had some characteristics that were typical of a specific epoch in church history. They symbolically and figuratively represent the Church Age from the time of the Book of Acts until the Rapture. Remember the theme of the Book of Revelation is the story of the Church. Our interpretation will be consistent with that theme. It is not the story of the nations. It is not the story of the Jews. It is the story of the Church. It begins in the Book of Acts with the Church of Ephesus.

Revelation 2:1-7
Ephesus The Primitive Church
AD 33 - AD 100

This is the same church to which Paul wrote the Book of Ephesians. The Apostle Paul had been the missionary-pastor of this congregation. It was an exciting, vibrant, evangelistic church that reached out, not only to the city of Ephesus, but to the hundreds of towns and villages of the entire region.This church was the hub of Paul's missionary endeavors. The history of the Church of Ephesus is a thrilling story of missions. We read about it in the Book of Acts.

Fifty years after Paul pastored in Ephesus John chose that church to represent the "Primitive Church" of the Apostolic period. At the time John wrote, the members of the congregation were no longer Aquila and Priscilla and other converts of Paul. The church was now made up of second and third generation Christians; and their love, zeal and fervor had cooled. Jesus said about them, "I have somewhat against thee because thou hast left thy first love."

Christ also had a positive comment to make about this early church of the first century. "Thou hatest the deeds of the Nicolaitans, which I also hate." The word Nicolaitan means in Greek **Nico** "to conquer" and **laitan** "laity." This was the beginning of the priesthood. Designated individuals outside of the congregation were taking control of the church. The early church was self governed. It was not part of some hierarchy. The pastor was generally selected from the congregation.Those churches had a very loose relationship to Paul, their missionary-pastor. They were not dominated by a power structure. But that was beginning to change by the end of the first century.

Revelation 2:8-11
Smyrna   The Persecuted Church
AD 100 - AD 312

The Christian Church of the first century enjoyed much popularity and acceptance. The persecution that it did receive came mostly from the Jewish community and was more a doctrinal-religious struggle than it was political. By mid-century the Christian Church had spread across the Roman empire. Rome was beginning to see the Christians as a threat, and proposed to stamp them out of existence. The easy times were about to end for the church.   Rome intended to annihilate it.

The Church of Smyrna represents the persecution that extended from about 100 A.D. to 312 A.D.The persecution and carnage that the Church suffered during this period of history has never been equaled. We read of the ordeal in **Fox's Book of Martyrs.** In Roman arenas Christians fought animals bare-handed to death. Fox writes that the coliseum of Rome was lit at night by the torches of oil-soaked Christians burning to death. During that time it was no longer possible for the Christians to practice their faith in public worship. Instead the believers in Rome worshiped clandestinely in the catacombs of the hills surrounding the city. Not only in Rome was the persecution felt, but throughout the entire Roman empire. The city of Rome burned while Nero was emperor and the blame was laid on the

Christians. In retaliation Jerusalem was sacked and the temple totally destroyed in the year AD 70.

God was aware of the pain and destruction that the believers endured. Jesus told that congregation that He was well aware of their suffering, their tribulation, and their poverty. In 2:10 He said that it was not Nero or some Roman governor nor any Roman centurion who was persecuting the Church. He named the source of their persecution....."the devil shall cast you into prison."

Revelation 2:12-17
Pergamos   The Church of Compromise
AD 312 - AD 540

After years of bloodbath and horrendous slaughter of Christians, the Ceasars of Rome changed their tactics. They sought a compromise with the Christian community. Rome, rather than Jerusalem and Alexandria, became the head-quarters city of Christianity. The church became part of the state, sharing the power and prestige of Rome. That was the beginning of what exists today as the Roman Catholic Church.

In 312 AD Emperor Constantine converted to Christianity and became the great benefactor of the Roman Catholic Church. In the fervor of his new found faith Constantine obligated the heathen barbaric nations he conquered to convert as well. He marched the heathen captives wholesale through rivers of baptism, and Rome became a "Christian" empire. The Roman Church became a powerful influence for good in that empire.

Jesus spoke well of the early Roman Catholic Church. "Thou holdest fast my name and hath not denied the faith," He said in Revelation 2:13. Even so, the church was in a precarious position of compromise. Their headquarters was right "where Satan's seat was." It is evident that Christ did not consider the Roman empire to be Christian in spite of its partnership with the church. That relationship of church and state is compared in 2:14 to the doctrine of Balaam. The reference is to the Old Testament account of a heathen ruler who sought religious support. This unhealthy relationship between church and state was later called the unholy alliance.

In 2:15 we can already sense drastic changes in the church as a result of this move toward Rome. The change had to do with the government of the church. The Church of Ephesus had deplored the Nicolaitans who had wanted to establish a priesthood, a hierarchy of clergy separate from the laity. The Church of

Pergamos embraced that doctrine and gave us the first Pope and Priests within the Christian movement. This was a church far removed from what the Apostle Paul had pastored.

I am not being critical and judgmental of the Roman Catholic Church, Keep in mind that when the Bible refers to the Church of Jesus Christ it is not referring to the Roman Catholic Church nor to any Protestant denomination. The church of Christ is the body of true believers and it is found in all seven churches of Revelation chapters two and three. Therefore, when we interpret this Scripture and identify the Roman Catholic Church we are only referring to the earthly organization. When we say that the Book of Revelation is the story of the church, we are not referring to any earthly denomination, but to that body of true believers who are within those organizations.

Revelation 2:18-39
Thyatira   The Church of the Middle Ages
AD 540 - AD 1517

The period of the Middle Ages, commonly referred to as the Dark Ages, was the age of the feudal lords. The church was the major landowner. This was when the massive cathedrals of Europe were built -- St. Peters, Notre Dame, Cologne and many others. The astronomical cost of those constructions was shared by the church and the state. Two church doctrines came into prominence at that time -- the doctrine of Purgatory and the doctrine of Indulgences. Both served to raise the tremendous revenue required to pay for the construction of those great cathedrals. It was the commercial aspect of the sale of indulgences and the sale of other ecclesiastical favors that prompted Martin Luther to begin his struggle for reform within the Church of Rome. That reform movement dealt with another issue that had become a problem in the Church of Thyatira. It was the use of images in worship.

When Christ sent this message to the angel of the congregation representing the Church of the Middle Ages, He had something very significant to say concerning the practice of idolatry introduced with the veneration of saints. Christ likens what happened in the Roman Catholic Church to another period of Biblical history when Ahab married Jezebel and eventually built idols and altars for the worship of her foreign gods. It was the first time that idolatry had been introduced into the Jewish community. Idolatry had always been an enemy without -- now it was an enemy within. Christ said to the Church of Thyatira that

He was angered by what Jezebel had done and with what was happening now at Thyatira. Unless the church repented of that practice of idolatry, the worship of images, it would be left to suffer the great tribulation. We will encounter this sin of Jezebel later in our study of the Tribulation.

A STUDY OF THE BOOK OF REVELATION

DIVISION TWO

LESSON III

DIVISION TWO

**The Church on Earth
From Pentecost to the
Rapture**

Chapters 2 and 3

REVELATION CHAPTER THREE

**Revelation 3:1-6
Sardis The Church of the Reformation
1517 - 1750**

The history of the Christian church continues. The church became more and more corrupt and powerful. Jesus said, "I know you have a name." They did. The church had become a significant part of society.Jesus said too that it was a church that thought it was alive, but it was dead. (Revelation 3:1) In Rev 3:3 the Lord urges the church to repent and reform. However, as bad as the church was, it was not totally corrupt. Christ recognized that within the priesthood and laity there were "a few names even in Sardis which have not defiled their garments."

We know some of the names to whom Jesus referred. Among them Luther, Knox, Zinzindorf, Tyndale, Wyclifff, Calvin. They pressed for repentance and reformation, but their voices went unheeded. They had no recourse but to leave the Church. The Reformation began.

The old church went on. It finished the construction of the mighty cathedrals. Out of its monasteries and seminaries came priests and monks who were kept ignorant of the Word. In contrast, the new stream of the church was a church founded on the open, understandable Word of God. The course of the true church of Jesus Christ diverted from the traditional Roman Church and became the missionary evangelistic church of the nineteenth century.

Revelation 3:7-13
Philadelphia   The Church of Modern Missions
1750 - 1950

Of the seven churches selected by Christ to

represent the Church Age, only the Church of Philadelphia was without one negative commentary. That was the Church before whom Christ set an open door that no man could shut. Through that door marched C. T. Studd, David Livingston, William Carey, and hundreds of other less known evangelical missionaries who with zeal and fervor carried the message of Christ to India, Africa, South America, China and to the islands of the sea. We live close enough to that Christian epoch that many of us today know personally some of those to whom Christ referred in this message to the Church of Philadelphia.

Revelation 3:14-22
Laodicea   The Church of the Last Days
1950 - The Rapture

Laodicea is the liberal, modernistic, socialized and dying church of the last days before the Rapture. Of course Laodicea does not typify all the Christian communities of believers. The Church of Ephesus continues to this day in evangelical congregations of believers which take the pattern for their doctrine, liturgy and government from the Book of Acts. In areas of the world dominated by atheistic or Moslem governments Christians are suffering today the same persecution as the Church of Smyrna. The Roman Catholic Church as it began with the Church of

Pergamos and continued through the Middle Ages as the Church of Thyatira exists today in basically the same format. The Reformation introduced by the Church of Sardis continues its efforts of reform. The missionary endeavors of the Church of Philadelphia will continue until the coming of the Lord.

However, it was the "mainline modernistic liberal churches" of today to whom the Lord was speaking when He addressed the Church of Laodicea. This was a church that was neither hot nor cold -- an ecumenical church that soft pedaled every doctrine that might be considered dogmatic or offensive to any segment of society. It was a church that wanted to embrace the world, and included in its body every religious belief. That church will be represented by the World Council of Churches. It is the ecumenical church which will soon encompass the Roman Catholic Church, some Eastern religions, as well as the majority of mainline Protestant denominations. It is the church that will become the vehicle for the false prophet of the tribulation.

In Revelation 3:20 we see Christ outside the door knocking, seeking entrance. He is too controversial a figure to be included in the Church of Laodicea. For the most part this church denies the virgin birth, the divinity of Christ, the person and work of the Holy Spirit, the demands of the Gospel, the eternal punishment of hell and the resurrection and future rewards of the believers. It is no wonder that Christ finds himself standing outside the door, rejected and forsaken. This is the church of which Jesus spoke when He raised the question, "Nevertheless, when the Son of Man returns, will He find faith on the earth?"

This Christ forsaking, dead Church of Laodicea is the last of the seven Churches. It represents the period of history that ushers in the Rapture and the Tribulation. These seven churches encompass 2000 years of history and bring us to the modern day in which you and I live.

Those 2000 years from John's experience on the Island of Patmos to the Rapture have seemed like a long time. That period of history is incorporated in the phrase recorded in Revelation 1:19. "The things thou hast seen" (past) "the things which are" (present) and "the things which are to come" (future) At the time John wrote this Book, the past, described as "the things which thou hast seen" was from AD 100 back to the Book of Acts 60 years earlier. The present "the things which are" was the church as it existed in AD 100, the Church of Smyrna. It was the church undergoing persecution under Nero. John himself was experiencing that persecution in his exile on the Isle of Patmos. "The things which are to come" the future, was all the 2000 year history of the church from 100 AD to the Rapture.

For us living in the twentieth century, the present is the Church of Laodicea, the last of the churches, the end of the Church Age.That church is symbolic of the church at the time of the Rapture. The past is the entire 2000 years of church history from the Book of Acts until the present. The future, the time period that remains before the Rapture, might be very brief.

We live every day expecting the imminent return of Christ. He could return for His church at this very moment -- even today as I write these words, or as you read them.   No prophecy remains to be fulfilled before the Lord returns. All that being true, my friend, we are not talking about a future society thousands of years away. The events we are studying could take place within the next seven years. If Jesus should return today for His church, there will follow seven years of Tribulation. At the conclusion of those seven brief years Christ will return to earth to begin His millennial reign. The next great event in church history will be the Rapture.

In chapter four that Rapture occurs. That chapter is also the beginning of a new division of the Book of Revelation.We must look at those divisions on the chart that outlines our study. That chart will reveal an extremely important key that has been overlooked in most studies of this Book. It has to do with the chronology of John's writings.

Examine the chart and you will discover that the study divides itself into seven logical divisions. Three of these divisions are parallel to each other to indicate that the events described in Division Three, Division Four and Division Five occur simultaneously. All three of these divisions cover the same time span from the Rapture to the Second Coming.

Most Bible studies on the Book of Revelation ignore this very important key to interpretation, and their oversight leads to a great deal of confusion. I have read many such Bible courses, and I have read scores of books interpreting Revelation. None of them have given me a satisfactory explanation as to why there are four battles of Armageddon described in chapter nine, fourteen, sixteen and finally again in chapter nineteen. Their interpretation of the sequence of events is very confusing. To me the plagues of the trumpets and bowls appear to be describing the same events. However, I have yet to find a Bible commentary that recognizes that fact.

••

**Chart of the Chronological Sequence
Of the Book of Revelation.................**

<u>DIVISION ONE</u>
John imprisoned on the Island of Patmos approximately 100 AD.

<u>DIVISION TWO</u>
The Church Age from Pentecost to the Rapture.

<u>DIVISION THREE</u>
The Church and the Tribulation as seen by John in heaven. From the Rapture to the 2nd Coming.

<u>DIVISION FOUR</u>
The Church and the Tribulation as seen by John on earth. From the Rapture to the 2nd Coming.

<u>DIVISION FIVE</u>
The satanic church of the False Prophet on earth from the Rapture to the 2nd Coming.

<u>DIVISION SIX</u>
We rebuild this planet Earth during the 1000 years of the Millennium.

<u>DIVISION SEVEN</u>
Eternity
••

		DIVISION THREE Saints organized in heaven to evangelize and administer judgment on earth The Rapture to the Second Coming Chapters 4-5		
DIVISION ONE John's encounter with Jesus Christ Chapter 1	DIVISION TWO The Church Age Seven Churches Pentecost to the Rapture Chapters 2-3	DIVISION FOUR Tribulation Church The rise of Antichrist and the False Prophet Rapture to the 2nd Coming Chapters 12-16	DIVISION SIX The Millennium We restore the earth and rule with Christ in the Kingdom Age 1000 years Chapters 19-20	DIVISION SEVEN The Holy City Millennium Forever Chapters 21-22
		DIVISION FIVE Satanic church Babylon destroyed Rapture to the 2nd Coming Chapters 17-18		

Many of the confounding riddles of the Book of Revelation are resolved when you discover that John is not writing a continuous story from chapter one through twenty two. There are three different accounts that John gives us covering the period of time from the Rapture to the Second Coming. The single most important discovery I have made in my study of Prophecy is that the Book of Revelation is not written chronologically.

The confusion I stumbled through before I made this enlightening discovery is the same bewilderment a new Christian would experience reading the account of the life of Christ as recorded in the first four divisions of the New Testament. It would seem apparent to the reader that Christ was crucified and resurrected four times. That dilemma has an obvious solution. The story of the death of Christ is told four times from four different points of view. It is this discovery that I have made concerning the Book of Revelation. Look again at the chart and we will briefly summarize these three parallel divisions.

DIVISION THREE   In chapters four through eleven, John is in heaven and describes the scene in heaven as the church is welcomed home at the Rapture, and then organized to participate in God's program for the seven years of the Tribulation. In these chapters of Division Three John also describes events transpiring on earth as seen from heaven.

DIVISION FOUR   Chapter twelve begins again at the Rapture and tells the story of the saints on earth and the interaction of that church with the saints in heaven. Yes, there will be a true church on earth that will go through the Tribulation. How many times has the question been asked -- "Will the church go through the Tribulation?" Bible students have been divided on both sides of this question. Many argue that the church will not go through the Tribulation on earth and others argue that it will. The truth is both are right. Every Christian who is walking in victory at the instant of the Rapture will be caught up to be with the Lord. However, there will be hundreds of thousands of professing Christians who will be left behind as were the five foolish virgins. Many of those will repent and find forgiveness after the Rapture. They will be the body of believers on earth and their numbers will increase to a multitude of many millions -- so great a multitude that they cannot be numbered. Chapters twelve through sixteen recount the experiences of those believers on earth from the Rapture to the Second Coming.

DIVISION FIVE   There is another story that threads through these seven years of the Tribulation. It is the account of the counterfeit or satanic false church represented by the prostitute woman in chapters seventeen and eighteen. This is the worldwide church directed by the false prophet from Rome. Throughout the Book of Revelation there is a clash between these two bodies; the true church of Jesus Christ and the false church of Satan.

The entire Book of Revelation is the story of the church. Division three is the church raptured into heaven. Division four is the church on earth composed of those who repent and are saved after the Rapture. Division Five is the false church of the false prophet. It is so important in this study to be constantly aware that the subject matter of Revelation is the church. It is not the story of Antichrist and his empire. Neither is it the story of the Jews, nor any other nation or confederation of nations. Antichrist, the Jews, the world powers and world politics are dealt with only as these persons and activities relate to the church. The Book of Revelation is the continuing saga of the church that began in the Book of Acts. Keeping that one thought in mind will guard you against many fallacious interpretations.

We are now ready to study chapter four -- THE RAPTURE.

THE BRIGHT SIDE OF THE APOCALYPSE

LESSON IV

DIVISION THREE

The saints organized in heaven to evangelize and administer judgment on earth during the Tribulation

Chapters 4 – 11

REVELATION CHAPTER FOUR
THE RAPTURE

The word "rapture" does not appear in the Bible, yet millions of Bible believing Christians have anticipated this event for centuries. The scriptural term is the "snatching up" or "the catching away" of the church. Paul describes the Rapture in this fashion.

For the Lord himself shall descend from heaven with a shout, with the voice of the archangel and with the trump of God, and the dead in Christ shall rise first.

Then we which are alive and remain shall be caught up together with them in the clouds to meet the Lord in the air, and so shall we ever be with the Lord. Wherefore, comfort one another with these words.

I Thessalonians 4:16-18

Let me clarify one thing. We must distinguish between the Rapture of the church and the Second Coming. When we confuse these two events it can only result in error in interpretation. The Second Coming of Christ occurs at the end of the seven years of Tribulation when Christ will return with millions of His saints as a glorious conqueror. "And every eye shall see Him." But at the Rapture He comes as a "thief in the night." Jesus told His disciples:

But of the day and the hour knoweth no man, not the angels which are in heaven, neither the Son, but the Father.
Take heed. Watch and pray, for ye know
not when the time is.

Mark 13:32,33

The most guarded secret of the universe is the day and the hour of the coming of the Lord at the Rapture. Later in our study we will discover the reason for this extreme secrecy. It is no secret that Christ is coming. This is no new doctrine. The church has been looking for His return since that moment on the Mount of Olives when the disciples saw Jesus Christ ascend into Heaven and disappear in the clouds, and heard the angel say:

Ye men of Galilee, why stand ye gazing up into heaven? This same Jesus which is taken up from you into heaven shall so come in like manner as ye have seen Him go into Heaven.

Acts 1:11

When the disciples left that hillside it became their custom to greet each other with the salutation, "The Lord is coming." The other would respond, "Yes, He is coming soon." It was their hope and expectation that Christ would return in their day. When the Apostle Paul wrote of the Rapture he said, "... and **we** which are alive and remain..." as though he fully expected to be one of those to be alive at Christ's coming. However, the years have past and the scoffers have come as Peter predicted. We no longer greet each with "the Lord is coming." We are aware that He is coming, however, we have lost the alertness of expectancy. Complacency and indifference -- these are the signs of the last days. The church needs to be awakened.

Most of what Jesus said about the signs of the end of the age were directed to the church and not the world. We have missed the message of the parables of the coming of the Lord because we fail to recognize that Jesus was talking about the attitude of the church toward His coming. His concern was not the attitude of the unbelievers, the children of darkness. An example of this error is how we have depicted the teaching of Christ in Matthew 7:13

Enter ye in at the straight gate, for wide is the gate and broad is the way that leadeth to destruction and many there be which go in thereat.

Matthew 7:13

I have often seen pictures drawn to depict what Jesus described. The artist showed a broad road of sin. You could see in the picture the drunkards and harlots plunging headlong into hell; while on the narrow lonely path a solitary pilgrim could be seen struggling up the hill on his way to the city of light.

That is not the message of this parable. Jesus is talking about the church. He is not describing the world. These are people who enter the gate looking for the way to happiness and peace. Even so, within that body called the church there are those who would broaden the way, lower the standards, lessen the demands and make the Christian's walk less restrictive. The Sermon on the Mount was preached for the church. This parable from that sermon is a warning to those of the church, a warning that a great many   people whose names are on the membership rolls are not ready for His coming. Look at another parable.

In that night there shall be two people in one bed. The one shall be taken and the other left. Two women shall be grinding together. The one shall be taken and the other left. Two men shall be in the field. The one shall be taken, and the other left.

Luke 17:34, 36

Note that Jesus does not say "one shall be with a harlot and the other with his wife and children" or "one will be committing acts of violence and the other acts of mercy." The message is not to the lost, but to the saved. It is not a message to the sinner, but to the redeemed. It is not a message to the unbeliever, but to the believer. The warning is for the church to be ready.

The parables of the servants awaiting the return of the Master carry this thought of readiness. There are several such parables of Christ. In the parable of the talents (Matthew 25:14-30) all those who received the talents were servants. When the Master returned, two of them were ready, and were rewarded for their faithfulness. The other was "cast outside in the darkness where there will be weeping and gnashing of teeth."

In the parable of the ten virgins (Matthew 25:1-3) the difference between the wise and foolish virgins is not a question of wickedness, but of readiness at the bridegroom's coming. Hear the tragic words, "And the door was shut." Christ welcomed five of the virgins to the wedding feast. The five foolish were shut out.

What is Jesus telling us about the Rapture in these parables of pilgrims, servants and virgins? His words are very sobering warnings to the church. Perhaps a modern parable might help us to understand.

There was a certain pastor who loved the Lord and served Him devotedly. Although he was a good man, evil temptation confronted him continually. Many times he had fallen prey to lustful fantasy. Every time he fell he repented, and God in His infinite mercy forgave and restored him. On one occasion the pastor yielded to the temptation to gratify the lustful imaginations of his heart and something unexpected happened. He was sitting in his study looking at suggestive pictures in an

unsavory magazine when the trumpet sounded and Christ appeared in the heavens. Many members of the pastor's congregation were raptured. His wife and children were suddenly ushered into the presence of the Lord. What of the pastor caught in the act of sinful disobedience? He was not even aware that the Rapture had taken place and that he was still on earth to face the terrible Tribulation.

There are preachers who would tell us that it doesn't matter how we live. The Rapture will catch up Christians from movie theaters and dance halls, and even from the arms of prostitutes. No, my friend, only those who are walking in obedience and readiness will meet the Lord in the air.

We can illustrate what will happen at the Rapture another way. How often have you run a traffic light as it switched from amber to red? You felt so lucky. You hadn't hit anyone and no traffic officer saw what you did to give you a ticket. You broke the law and got away with it. That is the way it is in the life of the Christian. He sins and gets away with it because God is so merciful that no matter how often he asks Him, He will forgive him. At the Rapture he will be caught. Only those who are ready will go. This is why the Lord warns us time and time again just as Paul does in I Thessalonians 5:23 --

... may your whole spirit, soul and body be preserved blameless at the coming of the Lord.

I Thessalonians 5:23

When John writes of the hope of His coming he says in I John 7:3

Everyone that hath this hope in him purifieth himself even as He is pure.

I John7:3

Nothing should call the church to a life of holiness like the hope and the uncertainty of the day of the Rapture. Paul speaks of this holiness when he writes to Timothy.

... keep this commandment without spot, unrebukeable until the appearing of our Lord Jesus Christ.

I timothy 6:14

Read these sobering words in Titus:

....teaching us that denying ungodliness and worldly lusts we should live soberly, right-eously and godly in this present world. Looking for that blessed hope and the glorious appearing of the great God and our Saviour Jesus Christ.

Titus 2:12,13

Friend, I want to be one of those waiting and ready for the appearing of our Lord Jesus Christ. Don't let that day overtake you in a moment of disobedience and sin. There will be no chance to get ready. His coming will be in an instant. The word in Greek is "atamo" from which we, of course, get our word atom, the infinitesimal division of matter. There will be no time to repent and no time to say, "I'm sorry." There will be no time to rid yourself of the filth of this world and no opportunity to find forgiveness. He will come in an instant, in the twinkling of an eye; and those who are ready will enter.

If the thought of the sudden and surprising Rapture and the impending judgment of those who are not ready strikes fear in your heart, that fear should drive you to your knees in true and sincere repentance. The true Christian has no fear of the future. It is a glorious future that God has prepared for those who love Him. When he sees the signs of the impending judgment of this world, the believer is to rejoice for "his redemption draweth nigh." Again we see the bright side of the Apocalypse.

Let us get back to the Apostle on the Isle of Patmos as he is about to experience the Rapture.

Revelation 4:1-3
The Voice Like a Trumpet
"Come Up Here."

Most often when we think of the Rapture our thoughts go to what will happen here on earth when millions of Christians are instantly and simultaneously snatched up to heaven. In chapter twelve we will return to the account of the Rapture and see the impact that will be felt on earth as the Christians are taken away. However, in chapter four John takes us first to that glorious meeting in the air and that marvelous welcome into heaven.

Remember the scene at the beginning of Revelation chapter four. John was alone on the island of Patmos worshipping. It was during that service that he heard the voice like a trumpet. It was on the island of Patmos where he saw the vision of the seven churches and their pastors held in the right hand of Jesus. Clearly John is on earth throughout the first three chapters of the Revelation.

Immediately following the vision of the seven churches John hears a voice from heaven that sounds like a trumpet. It is none other than Jesus Christ saying, "Come up here." The way John expressed what happened next is in these words, "At once I was in the Spirit and there before me was a throne in heaven and someone was sitting on it."

When you read Revelation 4:2 you discover that John is no longer on earth on the Isle of Patmos. Where is he? He is standing before a throne. Where is that throne? It is in heaven. Incredible as it may seem, John has experienced the Rapture. He became a type of the church caught up to meet the Lord. This is not a vision. John was literally caught up, raptured into heaven. The Apostle Paul wrote of a similar experience in II Corinthians 12:2-4.

I knew a man in Christ about fourteen years ago (whether in the body I cannot tell, or whether out of the body I cannot tell, God knoweth) such an one caught up to the third heaven.
And I knew such a man (whether in the body or out of the body I cannot tell. God knoweth.
How he was caught up into paradise and heard unspeakable words which it is not lawful for man to utter   II Corinthians 12:24

The place where John and Paul went was the same. The Apostle Paul was "caught up to the third heaven" and John is there in chapter four. The first heaven is the blue sky above us, the earth's atmosphere. The second heaven is the realm of heavenly bodies; the sun, the moon and the stars. The third heaven is the abode of God.

Although the place they went to was the same, the experiences of Paul and John were not identical. The difference was that Paul went to heaven in 30-40 AD whereas John was projected 2000 years into the future and arrived the day of the Rapture. The exciting thing about the Book of Revelation is that when John looks out over the sea of humanity before the throne he sees the redeemed of all ages. John could have identified you and me if he had looked closely. We were there in that crowd. That is beautiful.

When I look at the spectacular photograph of our planet Earth taken some years ago by our astronauts standing on the moon I am over-whelmed. In reality I am in that picture. Very clearly I can see the outline of the west coast of South America. On the day that photo was taken I was in Chile. I was involved in an evangelistic tent meeting revival in the city of Arica. If someone could enlarge that photo to give an adequate blow-up of that area of the desert in northern Chile, you might be able to distinguish this baldheaded missionary preaching the Gospel. Whether you can see me or not, I am there.

Have you ever attended a baseball game, seated high up in the grandstand. The TV camera pans over the crowd and they point the lens in your direction. Later in the week you are with friends in your living room watching a re-play of that event on TV. When they show that pan shot of the bleachers your eyes strain to find yourself in the picture of that crowd. Whether you can pick yourself out of the crowd you are there. You are on national television.

That is how I feel when I read the Book of Revelation. In nearly every chapter you and I are there. Whether you are caught up into heaven in the Rapture or miss it and are left behind on earth to go through the Tribulation, you will find yourself in scene after scene. The identical things that John is describing, you and I are there seeing them with him.

Remember this; the Book of Revelation is not an allegory. It is not a vision. It is not a dream. It is not a story told to John by angels. John was swept 2000 years into the future. He wasn't dreaming what he saw. He was there. God is eternal. He sees in panoramic view from the beginning to the end. With our vision we can see only the present and a few fragments of the past. God, however, is omniscient - all knowing.

I can illustrate what I mean by the Rose Parade. We stand on the curb of Colorado Boulevard in Pasadena and watch the spectacular floats pass by. We peer around the heads of other spectators but have a very limited view of what is happening. The floats pass and disappear. We are uncertain as to what is coming next. Look up in the sky at the blimp flying overhead. Can you imagine what a spectacular view we would have of the parade if we could look down from that airship? From there in the sky we would be able to see the parade from beginning to end.

That is similar to what happened to John, but what he experienced was more spectacular. God took John from the island of Patmos near the year 100 AD and projected him 2000 years into the future. He arrived in heaven at the moment of the Rapture, at the same instant that you and I along with millions of the redeemed of all ages arrive for our first fantastic sight of the throne of God and the glory of His presence.

As we continue through the Book of Revelation we will discover that we are there. We are living, functioning, performing in the scenes that John describes. We will be taking part in that fantastic experience about which we are studying. The Revelation tells me what I will be doing. John saw the future. He saw things that have not yet taken place. The identical scene that John describes, you and I will see one day soon. I wonder if after seeing it we will be able to describe it any better than what John has written. I doubt it. Paul was so aghast at the sight that he saw that he simply said that it was inexpressible. At least John made an effort to tell us what he saw.

I read John's description of the throne of God in Revelation 4:3 and remember the words of the Apostle Paul recorded in I Timothy 6:16. Paul wrote these words when he recalled that remarkable experience when he was caught up to the throne of God.

...God, the blessed and only ruler, King of kings and Lord of lords, who alone is immortal and lives in inapproachable light, whom no one has seen or can see.

I Timothy 6:16

John describes that same brilliance as if it were the reflection from a vast array of diamonds and emeralds and jewels of every kind. Our eyes will be dazzled at the brilliance of that same scene.

Revelation 4:4, 5
The Throne and Those Around It

When you read this descriptive chapter of that dazzling scene in heaven, remember John is not describing what he saw, but rather what was happening. What did he say? "Twenty four other thrones and seated on them were twenty four elders." I believe this refers to the twelve Patriarchs and the twelve Apostles who represent the leadership of both the Old and New Testament dispensations. Evidently those who were the leaders on earth will be the rulers in Heaven. This is consistent with the teaching of Christ in many parables.

Of course, the seven blazing lamps of Revelation 4:5 are the seven Spirits of God that we have already identified in Revelation 1:4 as the Holy Spirit. There is nothing mysterious about that.

Revelation 4:6-1
Saints and Angels

What else did he see? "There was what looked like a sea of glass, clear as crystal. The word "sea" is symbolic in the Bible for the "sea of humanity." We will find this symbol again in Revelation chapter 17. In Isaiah 17:12 the symbol refers to the nations as a "storm tossed sea." However, here in heaven, the storm is over. The sea is calm. It is John's way of expressing the peace of heaven.

"Around the throne were four living

creatures." (Revelation 4:6) Often we think of creatures as being some kind of lizard or some other repulsive slithering animal. The translation is unfortunate if it conveys that image. These are angelic beings with a very special ministry. They were probably very beautiful angels. There will be nothing repulsive about them when we see them. They will be the most beautiful angelic creatures we have ever seen. They are before the throne on several occasions, leading services of praise and worship. It is interesting to me that these four angelic beings reflect the four faces of Christ as depicted in the four Gospels. Matthew pictures Christ as the lion of the tribe of Judah. Mark depicts Him as the ox, the obedient servant. Luke represents Christ as the man. Christ in His humanity. John shows us Christ as the heavenly messenger represented by the eagle.

At the conclusion of the service of praise and worship led by those four angelic beings, the twenty-four elders, the leaders of the Old and New Testament take off their crowns and lay them before the throne saying -- "You are worthy, our Lord, to receive glory and honor and power."

You and I will be at that meeting in the air. You and I will be at that spectacular, overwhelming service of worship when we are welcomed into heaven. Neither Paul nor John could even attempt to describe the glory, the joy, the happiness, the emotion of that reunion when we are united with our loved ones, see our Lord and Saviour face to face, and join with angelic hosts singing anthems of praise to Christ our King.

I can now better understand the words of Scripture -

Eye hath not seen, nor ear heard, neither hath it entered into the heart of man the things which God hath prepared for those who love Him.

THERE IS A BRIGHT SIDE OF THE APOCALYSE

THE BRIGHT SIDE OF THE APOCALYPSE

LESSON V

DIVISION THREE

The saints organized in heaven to evangelize and administer judgment on earth during the Tribulation

Chapters 4 – 11

REVELATION CHAPTER FIVE

Revelation 5:1-14
The Sealed Scroll

This is the key chapter to the understanding of the Book of Revelation. The scene is as it was in Revelation chapter four. You and I are in that scene. We are in heaven shortly after the Rapture. We are witnessing the identical drama that John is about to describe. One day we will be a part of that "sea of humanity" looking on. We too will see a scroll in the right hand of the one who sits on the throne. We too will hear the mighty angel proclaiming in a loud voice, "Who is worthy to break the seal and to open the scroll?" We, too, will sense the sadness felt by John when no one is found to be worthy. Neither Abraham, Moses, Isaiah, Elijah, nor any of the apostles could touch that scroll. We too will weep with John because none was found worthy. The Worthy One is about to be discovered though. One of the twenty-four elders, possibly one of the apostles or a patriarch of the Old Testament tells John not to weep. "See the Lion of the tribe of Judah, the Root of David" We know who that is. It is Jesus. He is the triumphant one. He is the one who is worthy to break the seals and open the scroll.

Does this secret scroll seem like a vague mystery to you? Does this mysterious scene in heaven confuse you? Much misinterpretation of the Book of Revelation comes from not understanding the meaning of the seals and the scroll. What is the meaning of this drama? What is the significance of the scroll and the seven seals? If we can solve this mystery we will have the key to the unveiling of the entire Book of Revelation.

John knew what the scroll meant. He knew what the opening of the scroll signified. This was to be the "Redemption of the Purchased Possession." Paul speaks of in Ephesians 1:13,14.

Ye were sealed with the Holy Spirit of promise which is the earnest of our inheritance until the redemption of the purchased possession.

What is the redemption of the purchased possession? The term refers to the legal right of all Jewish citizens. In the event that any family was forced to sell its property for any reason, thus depriving its descendant from receiving the inheritance of that property; the law provided that such a property could be bought back, or redeemed, at any time by any member of the family. The Bible calls the procedure the Redemption of the Purchased Possession. In Jeremiah chapter 32 we have an example.

Here is how Jewish law outlined the procedure. Suppose my father was forced to sell our farm and home to pay off debts. At any time any heirs would have the right to buy back that farm at the price my father had sold it. The total transaction would be in two stages.

First I would go to the court to present my claim. I would take with me witnesses to verify my statements and to authenticate my claim. I would present to the court the bill of sale that my father had received when he sold the property and

I would pay to the court the purchase price. The judge would receive the money and write me out a document on which was written a description of the property, its location and its boundaries. The judge would write in the legal transfer of ownership to me. On the reverse side of the document the witnesses would place their signatures. The judge would then roll the document in the form of a scroll and seal it to prevent any tampering. When the judge hands me this document he declares me to be the legal owner of my father's farm and home. However, someone else occupies that property. He has built pig pens and chicken coops.He has crops planted and has no intention of leaving my farm voluntarily.

The next step I must take is to present this scroll to the present occupant and in the presence of the witnesses break the seals and declare to the occupant my rights of ownership and possession. If he still refuses to leave the land I have the backing and authority of the entire nation to effect my claim.I can resort to that legal action, if necessary, to evict him from my redeemed pro-perty. That process is the redemption of the purchased possession, and is exactly what hap-pens in heaven at the throne in Revelation chapter five. We will get back what we lost long ago.

When Jesus cried out at Calvary, "It is

finished."God had completed his plan of redemption. That redemption included (1) the redemption of our soul (2) the redemption of our body and (3) the redemption of our planet. That was 2000 years ago but Satan has not relinquished this earth. He continues to pollute this world with sin, immorality, and filth of every kind. Our beautiful home has been totally desecrated. What was once a beautiful world has been made a disgrace, unfit to be the dwelling place of God and His people. Two thousand years after Calvary there is much to be done to redeem this world.

First, God will evict Satan and will take possession of this planet for us. What takes place in Revelation chapter five before the throne of God is the second step in the process of the redemption of the purchased possession. Our Lord will break the seals and will forcibly evict Satan from this earth. Jesus Christ will clean up all the trash. He will purge from the earth every remembrance of Satan. The world will be restored to the condition it was at creation. He will remove completely whatever blight sin has caused. That will include the elimination of all weeds, thorns, disease, pestilence, pollution and contamination. The governments of this planet have spent billions of dollars to clean the air, wipe out disease and remove the contamination; but they have scarcely made even a minimal impact on the problem. God will completely clean up the environment when He restores this world.

Once we understand what is happening not much is left in chapter five that needs clarification. The scene is the emotion packed campmeeting service around the throne when our Lord and Saviour is declared the one and the only one worthy to break the seals and present to Satan proof that planet Earth was redeemed at Calvary.

THE BRIGHT SIDE OF THE APOCALYPSE

LESSON VI

DIVISION THREE

The seals are opened

Chapters 4 – 11

REVELATION CHAPTER SIX

THE FOUR HORSEMEN OF THE APOCALYPSE. Entire books have been written on the subject of these four horsemen. Who or what are they? Where do they come from? And what are they doing? I have read some bizarre interpretations of chapter six. It is incredible that intelligent well educated Bible scholars can read the same passage of Scripture and be so diverse in their interpretation of the meaning of the text. Because the information given in Revelation 6:2, describing the rider on the white horse is very limited, any interpretation of this passage will always be either speculative or subjective. It will not be an irrefutable conclusion. I have read virtually hundreds of interpretations of this chapter of the Bible to determine the points of disagreement between authors. Many of those authors are renowned Bible scholars whom you and I could depend upon for a sound doctrinal interpretation of other themes and passages of Scripture. I can only conclude from their writings concerning this chapter that some of those celebrated scholars are dead wrong since they cannot all be right and be so incongruent in their interpretation.

When I read what others have written and see the inconsistency and the confusion in their rendering of this passage, it gives me encouragement to write what I am about to present in this book, **The Bright Side Of The Apocalypse**. I may stand alone in my interpretation of the four horsemen of the Apocalypse. What I am going to suggest as to the identity of these characters may seem more bizarre than anything you have ever read. You are free to disregard my conclusions. What I am going to teach you, I believe to be the truth. That teaching will be consistent with what I see as the basic theme of Revelation -- the story of the church. The church consists of the saints, you and me.The plan of God involves us in a manner that you probably have never considered to be in the realm of possibility.

What happens in chapter six is very much related to that mysterious scroll we studied in chapter five. We saw the significance of the sealed scroll. It is Christ's legitimate claim to possession of our planet Earth. Satan is about to be expelled from this world; and you and I, the church, will be very much involved in that process of expulsion. Because they do not see this involvement most Bible teachers have a totally different interpretation of this chapter. There is one key thought that unravels the entire Book of Revelation. That key is the involvement of the saints in heaven and on earth during the seven years of the Tribulation. Chapter six is no exception. We see in this chapter the church, the saints, organized in heaven and directed by Christ to administer the judgment of God upon the earth.

Chapter six covers the time from the Rapture to mid-point in the Tribulation. It begins with these words:

I watched, John said, as the Lamb opened the first of the seven seals.   Revelation 6:1

Next, John related that one of those beautiful angels called him over to the banister of heaven where he could look down upon the earth.

What John described in chapter six was a scene of action taking place on earth as seen from the viewpoint of heaven. Later in chapter 12 John will be on earth and will give us the same account of what happens to the church during the Tribulation, but from the viewpoint of earth. The action involves four special horsemen who represent the church in its activities during the initial three and a half years of the Great Tribulation.

An angel spoke in Revelation 6:1. He said, "Come." To whom is he speaking? Is it to John, to the redeemed, or to the horsemen? The "come" could just as well be translated "go"-- more like, "Come on, Let's go." When the starter of a sack race stands at the finish line hollers "Go" he is really meaning "Come." In each of these verses 1, 3, 5 and 7 the angel was talking to the riders and the meaning is "Come and go. It is your turn."

Revelation 6:1, 2
The First Seal
The Rider on the White Horse

And I saw and behold a white horse, and he that sat on him had a bow; and a crown was given unto him and he went forth conquering and to conquer.

Revelation 6:2

Note how John described the rider on the white horse. He had a bow and a crown and he rode out as a conqueror bent on conquest. Who does this rider represent? I am fully aware that some prominent Bible interpreters believe that the rider of the white horse is the Antichrist. I cannot agree with that interpretation for a number of reasons:

In the first place, this rider was sent from heaven. It was in heaven that he mounted the white horse. It was in heaven that he received the bow and the crown before being sent to earth. Antichrist will not be sent from heaven. Antichrist will be a messenger of Satan and not of Christ. Certainly the symbols used do not support the idea that this was Antichrist, a demon possessed man set against God and His universe. White is the color representative of the redeemed. Also look at the bow he was given. That bow was not an instrument of war. There was no mention of arrows. It was a bow without arrows. That was a bow like the rainbow, which represented grace and mercy. The crown was the victor's crown that every believer will receive. The verse identified the rider as a conqueror, the believer who has fought the good fight of faith and has been given the crown of righteousness as Paul put it. This rider's mission was a mission of evangelism -- to conquer in the name of the Redeemer.

I suggested earlier that it will be possible to repent and to be saved after the Rapture. Not only will it be possible, a concentrated effort of evangelism will be made to preach the Gospel to the ends of the earth and millions will be saved.

The great commission given to the Church was "Go ye into all the world and preach the Gospel to every creature." I was a missionary for twenty-five years, evangelizing Latin America. I have labored in Cuba, Mexico, Peru, Bolivia, Uruguay, Argentina and Chile. From what I have seen of missionary work we are a long way from evangelizing every creature. The fact is that there are more heathen in the world today than when David Livingston first went to Africa and William Carey first went to India. More heathen are being born into the world every day than will ever be evangelized before the Rapture. Also there are entire nations of the world that are totally closed to the Gospel and will never be evangelized before the Lord returns at the Rapture.

Jesus said in Matthew 24:14 "This Gospel will be preached in the whole world as a testimony to all nations, then shall the end come." There are denominations that teach us that the impetus of world missions is to reach that last man, woman, boy or girl, with the Gospel; and when the last person has heard the Good News, Christ will return for His church. The error of that theology is this. In the statement Jesus made in both Matthew and Mark He is not referring to the Rapture, but to His Second Coming. The Second Coming is the return of Christ to earth. This will take place after the Tribulation.

When Christ speaks of the entire world, every individual, being evangelized, He is talking about an incredible task. It is a task that the Church set out to do in the first century and has not yet completed nearly 2000 years later. Could it be that this mission that has not been completed in 20 centuries will be accomplished in a mere three and a half years. Have you ever wondered who will evangelize the entire world and how will they do it? We see the results of that missionary effort in this chapter of Revelation. Verses nine through eleven is a scene in which John describes the souls of those who had been slain because of the Word of God and the testimony they maintained. Whoever these souls were the Lord told them to wait until the number of their fellow servants and brethren who were to be killed, as they had been, was completed. These obviously were not Christians at the moment of the Rapture. They were not a part of the bride of Christ that was caught up into heaven. Evidently they are believers who were saved and martyred after the Rapture. The martyrdom was to continue. Others were yet to be killed to complete their number.

In Revelation 7:9-17 we see another reference to these souls. Their number has now been completed. They are a multitude that no one could count, from every nation, tribe, people and language; standing before the throne in front of the Lamb dressed in white robes, holding palm branches in their hands. They are in heaven. Who are they?This was the question asked by John and answered by the angel. -- "These are they who have come out of the Great Tribulation. They have washed their robes and made them white in the blood of the Lamb."

The world will be evangelized during the Tribulation and millions will be saved -- a multitude that cannot be numbered. They are from every tribe of the jungles of South America and Africa and from the islands of the sea. They are from every nation -- Tibet, Outer Mongolia, Afghanistan, Iraq, Russia, China, Cambodia and every other nation of the world. They are from the countless nations that are closed to the Gospel and will never be evangelized before the Rapture. This multitude will come from every one of the more than 3000 languages spoken in the world today.The rider on the white horse represents whoever it is who carries on this mission of evangelism during the Tribulation. He represents those evangelists. But who are they? Who will evangelize the world? Who will be the missionaries and preachers of the Gospel who in three and a half years will accomplish under the most adverse circumstances what the church has not been able to do in 2000 years?

There is a reference to this evangelism in Revelation 14:5 -- "Then I saw another angel flying in midair and he had the eternal Gospel to proclaim to those who live on the earth, to every nation, tribe, language, and people." This is no angel. God never commissioned angels to preach the Gospel. This "angel" of Revelation 14:5 must represent a group of human beings who are commissioned to evangelize the entire world during the Tribulation. These evangelists are represented by the rider on the white horse in Revelation 6:1 and 2 and by the angel of Revelation 14:5. Both the angel and the rider on the white horse refer to the same evangelists. There are three possibilities as to who they might be.

As to the first possibility, there are those who say that the world will be evangelized by the new converts. Many of those who are left after the Rapture will repent and it will be those who will evangelize the world. It is true that many who are left will repent and will be converted. I know that if I were one of those who missed the Rapture I would seek a place of repentance. Most of those people will not be preachers, missionaries or evangelists but lukewarm church members ill-prepared for the task of world evangelism. Besides, they will be confronted with persecution and opposition, like no Christians have ever known. They will not be able to evangelize the world. There is no way that these post rapture converts are the evangelists.

Others say that the evangelists are the 144,000 Jews from the twelve tribes who were numbered and sealed in chapter seven of Revelation. It is true that these Jews who have accepted Jesus Christ as their Messiah probably would share their faith with others. However, from reading Matthew 24 and Revelation 7 it is evident that these are Palestinian Jews. They reside in the holy land. They are numbered and sealed midpoint in the seven years and told to flee and are given no instructions to evangelize. The truth is, by then the evangelism had been completed. During the first three and a half years the Gospel was preached to all who were going to be saved and there would be no preaching of the Gospel in the second half of the Tribulation. No, these 144,000 are not the evangelists. They are a chosen group of believers who will be scattered across the face of the earth. They will be the remnant of believers on earth to welcome Christ at the Second Coming, but in no way could they be those who will evangelize the world.

Then who are the evangelists? Read what the angel said to John in Revelation 10:11 --

Thou must prophesy again before many peoples, nations and tongues and kings.

Keep in mind that John was nearly 100 years old when the angel spoke those words to him, and that he died not many years after they were spoken. When was that promise to John to be fulfilled? When was he to preach again before many peoples, nations, tongues and kings? That promise has not yet been fulfilled, but it will be. John will be one of those evangelists who will be preaching the Word during the first three and a half years of the Tribulation. The only human beings who could ever complete that task of evangelism are the preachers, missionaries and evangelists. John and thousands of others of us are represented by the rider on the white horse. We will be commissioned in heaven to return to earth in our resurrected, immortal, spiritual bodies to go forth to conquer the world for Christ.

What a glorious thought! I expect to be back here on earth during the Tribulation period fulfilling my calling as a missionary; completing the work I never got done before the Rapture. Can you imagine the tremendous advantage I will have when I come back in a spiritual body? Don't be too quick to close your mind to such a possibility. I am sure you believe that at the Rapture our mortal bodies will be changed to immortal spiritual bodies. Of course you believe that immediately following the Tribulation all of us will be coming back from heaven to live on this planet for 1000 years during the millennium. All that being true, I do not find it absurd to accept that I could return to earth as an evangelist during the Tribulation.

I am not sure what all that implies. "But we know this." John said, "We shall be like Jesus, for we shall see Him as He is." (I John 3:2) We do have some knowledge as to what kind of body Christ had after His death and resurrection. It was a body capable of passing through solid walls, or entering the Upper Room through shut and bolted doors. With that body Jesus had the capability of leaving earth and going to heaven, then return to earth again in a matter of seconds or minutes. On the first Easter morning Christ met Mary in the garden and said to her, "Don't touch me. I have not yet ascended unto my Father." (John 20:17) It could not have been many minutes later that Christ met a group of women outside the garden and they clasped His feet and worshipped Him. (Matthew 28:8) Evidently between these two Easter morning encounters Christ had gone to heaven,however many millions of miles that might be, and returned to Earth. There are still other characteristics of a "spiritual body" that we learn from the appearances of Christ between the resurrection and the ascension. We discover that He is able to appear and disappear at will. He is able to assume another form of identity. (Mark 16:12) What excites me is that we shall be like Him.

When I went to the Amazon jungles with my family it was a time consuming perilous journey of many weeks. When I return in a spiritual body I will have no need for airplanes, trucks, mules and motor boats to take me to my field of labor. In an instant I will be any place on earth. I could be preaching the Word on a street corner in Buenos Aires when the police come to arrest me. In an instant I could be on another street corner, or in Bejing, China if that is where I was to be.

And what about language? There are 3000 tongues spoken on earth today. After years of study I have mastered English and Spanish. I learned a little French and German and gained some understanding of the language of the Aguaruna Indians in the Amazon. It is not easy to become fluent in a foreign tongue. Less than half of the 3000 languages spoken in the world today has been deciphered and written. The promise to John was that he would preach in many tongues. This new breed of missionary will have the capability of preaching with total fluency in any language of the world. We saw an inkling of that gift on the Day of Pentecost when the disciples preached in multiple languages to the amazement of those who heard them. We shall be like Jesus, the Word says, and He has no difficulty whatsoever communicating with any person on earth today, whatever language may be his.

It is not difficult to see the advantage we will have in the task of world evangelism. Not the least of these advantages is that we will be immortal. Neither Satan nor any of his forces under Antichrist can harm us. John calls us conquerors bent on conquest in Revelation 6:2. I can see no way that the formidable task of world evangelism could be achieved by any other human beings than those who return to earth in their spiritual bodies to do it. To me this is a fantastic revelation. What a privilege we will have. We will work side by side in the same mission of evangelism with Paul the Apostle, David Livingston, John Wesley, D. L. Moody, Nate Saint, Mother Theresa and hundreds of thousands of others who one day will invade this planet Earth commissioned to preach the Gospel to every tribe, nation, tongue and people. I expect too be a part of that glorious operation. It is unfortunate that many Bible teachers have overlooked the significance of the ministry of the rider on the white horse. These teachers seem to overlook the mission of world evangelism during the Tribulation.

Revelation 6:3, 4
The Second Seal
The Rider on the Fiery Red Horse

This time it was another of those four beautiful angels who calls John over to look and see -- "Another horse came out" he said, "a fiery red one" Its rider was given power to take peace from the earth and make men slay each other. The Lord gave him a great sword.

You cannot take peace from the earth unless there already is peace, and there will be. The Antichrist will be a man of peace. He will be Christ-like in many respects. He will not be a man of war. He will not be another Hitler or Stalin when he comes into power. I see Antichrist as being more like Dag Hammarskjold, the beloved secretary of the United Nations who was killed in recent years. He will be a diplomat capable of bringing warring nations to the peace table. He will do what no one has ever done -- heal the breech between the Jews and the Arabs. At the outset of the Tribulation period the world will be at peace. Jesus said, "Beware when they say peace and safety." It was this period of peace under Antichrist of which He spoke.

There will be peace and there will be prosperity as the world has never known. The leading world power then will not be Japan, the United States or Russia. Probably the core of the empire of Antichrist will be the European Common Market, and the man we are talking about will be the president of the European Economic Community. Bible scholars for years have agreed that the fourth kingdom of Daniel's vision was the Roman Empire. It was to be divided into two periods separated by the 2000 years of the Church Age. The ancient Roman empire is to be reconstructed in the last days and become the center of the rule of Antichrist. The make-up of the Common Market today parallels in an unbelievable way the area of the world that made up the ancient Roman empire.

We are not ignorant of what to expect in the immediate future of the world. The alignment of nations and the armament of world powers; the concentration of universal interest in the Middle East is not by chance, but by design. The Bible very well describes that design. Every Christian needs to have an understanding of the Word of

God so that these days should not overtake him unawares. That is the purpose of my writing this book. It is an effort to put into the hands of a few more people a clearer understanding of these marvelous revelations.

The Revelation tells us that sometime after the Rapture the man described to be antichrist will be revealed. It could very well be that the man who shortly will be that world leader is alive on earth today. He could be a university student. He may be a junior diplomat. It could be that he already is in the wings ready to step on stage and take his destined place as a world leader. Of this we can be certain -- God is in control of those circumstances that will bring this person to the forefront. It will be at the precise time for the fulfillment of these prophecies we are studying.

God is not only in control in an abstract way, but very much involved. His involvement comes through the church, His saints. The rider of the fiery red horse of Revelation 6:3,4 represents another group of saints organized in heaven and returned to earth in their immortal, supernatural bodies to carry on the task of taking peace from the earth.

I admit that much of what I will be telling you concerning the activities of these saints is speculation. It requires filling in the blanks, reading between the lines, using your imagination. There is nothing wrong with that. Any clear understanding of the Biblical accounts requires that we use our imagination.

Let me give you an example. In Mark 7:24 the Word says, "Jesus left that place and went to the vicinity of Tyre." In reading Mark 6 and 7 it is not difficult to establish that the place Jesus left from was the home of Peter in Capernaum. The point is this. Jesus left "that place" and went to the vicinity of Tyre. That statement involves a four day journey of which we are told absolutely nothing. Although the Scriptures give us no details of that trip we can assume that Jesus and His disciples walked from Capernaum to Tyre, a distance of more than 100 miles. The trip itself would have been somewhat of an adventure. I can very well imagine the scene of Jesus and His disciples preparing to start their journey very early one morning I recall similar trips that I have made on foot as a missionary in South America. I can still feel the cold wet dew of early morning as we walked through the high grass. I can recall the plans we made for those trips. I wonder what they took with them to eat and what provisions they made for sleeping the two or three nights on the trail.

I can imagine they planned their route to

take them through Jesus' home town of Nazareth and that they spent some time there with His family. The disciples probably bedded down in the old carpenter shop where Jesus had worked for so many years. Just thinking about it, I can almost smell the pungent odor of cedar shavings.

The next morning Jesus and His disciples were up early getting ready for their hike to the Mediterranean coast. They walked through lush green pastures. They crossed cascading brooks. They climbed rocky hills. They made their way through shaded woods. I can see the disciples skipping stones across meadow ponds. They talked. They laughed. They asked questions. They met people along the way. There are many interesting experiences that group had that were never recorded in the Scriptures. Mark does not tell us of the beauty of the blue Mediterranean as they came down out of the hills to the palm tree lined beaches. We don't know whether the disciples yielded to the temptation to plunge into the warm Mediterranean waters for a swim and a bath. I imagine that they did. Then they had that beautiful walk of several hours along the seashore north to Tyre.

All we are told in the Scripture is that, "Jesus left that place and went to the vicinity of Tyre." You miss much of the reality and excitement of reading the Bible if you are not able with your imagination to fill in between verses. It does no harm to the Scriptures to assume that such things as I described might have taken place. This is the kind of speculation I am doing in Revelation chapter six. In the case of the rider on the fiery red horse we only know what his mission was.We can only imagine how that mission was to be accomplished.

The mission of the church on earth is clearly stated in Matthew 28:18-20

All power is given unto me in heaven and in earth. Go ye therefore, and teach all nations baptizing them in the name of the Father, and of the Son, and of the Holy Ghost. Teaching them to observe all things whatsoever I have commanded you; and lo, I am with you always, even unto the end of the world.

After the Rapture the church will be given a different mission. It is stated in I Corinthians 6:2.

Do ye not know that the saints will judge the world?

There is a prophecy in Psalms 149:5-9 that sheds a bit more light on how we the saints are going to be involved in the administration of the affairs of this world.

Let the saints be joyful in glory; let them sing upon their beds. Let the high praises of God be in their mouths and a two edged sword in their hand. To execute vengeance upon the heathen and punishments upon the people; to bind their kings with chains, and their nobles with fetters of iron. To execute upon them the judgment written. This honor have all his saints. Praise ye the Lord.   Psalms 149:5-9

In Revelation 2:26 and 27 there is another clear prophecy of the same assignment given to the saints after the Rapture. We will be very much involved in the judgment of this world and in the expulsion of Satan from this earth. I believe that the prophecy of Psalms 149 will be fulfilled by the action taken by these saints represented by the rider of the fiery red horse. Their mission is to take peace from the earth. Who are these people represented by the rider on the fiery red horse?

They are very special saints organized in heaven for this mission of subversion on earth. We have seen how God developed a mighty corp of missionary-evangelists over the centuries and now returns them in force to planet earth to carry on a three and a half year mission of evangelism that will reach every tribe and nation and bring millions into the kingdom. I expect to be one of those evangelists. Now we see that God has been preparing a very special, group of people across the centuries who have the knack, the disposition, the know how, the expertise to return to earth in their immortal spiritual bodies to spread total havoc and confusion throughout the kingdom of Antichrist. Some of you who are reading this book will be a part of this very special team. There will be hundreds of thousands of you involved.   Your mission will be to infiltrate every sector of the economy. You will bring turmoil, strife, confusion which will cause rebellion, work stoppages, and every kind of domestic upheaval. This is not war. Yet the expression "he will make men slay each other" indicates that it will be a grave and serious involvement.

All of this is for a purpose. We know that the Christians here on earth are going to be subjected to very severe tribulation. The purpose of the plan involving the second horseman is to distract the forces of Antichrist and give the Christians and evangelists a reprieve. The peace and prosperity that ushers in the reign of Antichrist will not last. His fame and world acclaim will not last. God intervenes through the actions of those represented by the rider on the fiery red horse. The drama is exciting.

Maybe you are one of those who would

delight in being involved in such a project. Evidently the saints sent back here for this mission will enjoy their work. "They will rejoice in this honor and sing for joy on their beds." "The power of God will be in their mouths and a two edged sword in their hands." The "two edged sword" is the Bible. It is not simply a book. It is God's WORD. That two-edged sword, or the Word, is the authority that God gives these saints to enable them to accomplish their unique mission.

I can hear some of you saying, "I can't see myself in that role." In that case, my friend, you probably will not be one of this special force. However, there are thousands of believers God is preparing for this involvement "to inflict vengeance on the nations and punishment on the people, to bind the kings with fetters and the nobles with shackles of iron, to carry out the sentence written against them." (Psalm 149) It is not difficult for me to imagine how they will perform that task.

For much of my life I lived in the third world countries of South America and experienced first hand the havoc a few communist cadres could cause when they were placed in strategic positions in universities, labor unions, industries, hospital staffs, city government and the military forces. That very small percentage of the general population had the power to call strikes and work stoppages, to cause walkouts and sitdowns that brought the economy of country after country to a complete standstill. It is this kind of strife that is described by the mission of the rider on the red horse. "He was given power to take peace from the earth."

Revelation 6:5, 6
The Third Seal
The Rider Of The Black Horse

Here we learn of another group of saints organized in heaven and returned to earth with another mission. Their assignment comes about as a direct result of the strikes and strife caused by those who infiltrated labor, government, education and industry as represented by the rider on the red horse. Shortages and the beginning of famine develop as a direct result of these insurmountable labor problems and work stoppages. I have already seen in my lifetime that which is described in Revelation 6:5,6. During the years we lived in Uruguay we saw what happens when industry is brought to a halt by work stoppages and general strikes. The shelves of the supermarkets were soon bare. We would wait in line for hours for the chance to buy a liter of milk, a few scraps of meat, a kilo of flour or a pound of sugar.

What would happen in a city like Los

Angeles if there were a complete shutdown of all transportation, all communications, all utilities, all services, and all industry? No food could be brought in. All services would be stopped. Hospitals would be closed. Nothing would function. Within a few weeks there would be uncontrollable havoc. When nothing is replaced on supermarket shelves, those shelves would soon be empty. Fruit and produce would be left in the fields to rot. Not a truck, a train or a ship would move. Millions of people would panic and riot. I saw it happen in a city of two million people, and it is a terrible thing.

This is what is being reported in Revelation chapter six. Those who are represented by the rider on the black horse do not cause the famine. The Lord sends this group to earth to administer a system of rationing and food distribution. What happens during this period of the Tribulation appears to be havoc, but in reality it is a well organized and controlled plan of God. We will be very much involved in that plan. By we I mean you and me. The purpose of this plan and design is to facilitate the preaching of the gospel and to distract Antichrist from his set purpose of persecuting and destroying the church on earth.

Revelation 6:7, 8
The Fourth Seal

The Rider of the Pale Horse

The rider of the fourth and last horse is death itself. This is no mystery. Verse eight clearly states it. I am not certain just how the saints will be involved in the mission of this fourth horseman, but we will be.

People will die by the millions. The Word tells us of four ways by which they will die. These verses tell us that one fourth of the world's population will die during this period. Today that would be more than a thousand million people. How will they die? John tells us (1) by the sword, which will probably be by police action to quell the inevitable violence and riots caused by the food shortages and resulting famine. These rioting crowds will be mercilessly mowed down by the armies and police force of Antichrist. (2) Millions will die of the famine itself. They will starve to death. (3) Millions more will die from plagues and disease caused by these circumstances. Plague always follows famine. Death will be so common that it will be impossible to keep up with the burial of the dead. An uncontrollable plague will result. (4) The fourth way that millions more will die will be by the "wild beasts of the earth." John is not here talking about lions and wolves. He is referring to household pets -- dogs and cats that will turn into ravenous beasts due to the famine and starvation. John is talking about billions of rats that now feed on the city garbage, but when there is no more garbage they will turn on the human population in a nightmare of horrible carnage. A total of more than a billion people will die these violent excruciating deaths. The metropolitan areas will feel most of the effect of this strife and famine while vast rural sections of the world will not at all be affected by these plagues.

It certainly will not be easy to be a Christian in those days. Tremendous pressure will be brought against the believers to denounce their faith.Any persons identified as Christians will be martyred. We see these martyred saints as the fifth seal is broken in Revelation 6:9.

Revelation 6:9-11
The Fifth Seal
The Souls of the Martyrs

When we get to chapters twelve and thirteen we will see in John's account what is happening on earth as a result of the operation of these four horsemen. Thousands of those who were left on earth after the Rapture have repented and have found forgiveness. We will see the work of the evangelists sent from heaven. They will win virtually millions to Christ. None of this goes unnoticed by Antichrist and his cohort the false prophet.

They devise the satanic plan of the mark of the beast requiring everyone on the face of the earth to sell his soul or face imminent death at the hands of the Antichrist's death squads. Even so the Christians continue to multiply through the effective ministry of the saints sent from heaven to evangelize. Thousands of other saints are sent to earth to occupy strategic government positions responsible for the entire program of food rationing. These are the saints represented by the rider on the third horse. Hundreds of thousands of other saints from heaven will be here to thwart the schemes of Antichrist and the false prophet by causing strife and turmoil. The ministry of these saints sent back from heaven will alleviate much of the pressure on the Christians on earth. Even so, the persecution is devastating. There is a literal war waged against the Christians. Antichrist and the false prophet will be satisfied with nothing less than the complete extermination of the Christian church on earth. Hundreds of thousands and even millions of Christians will be martyred.

It is these martyrs that John sees and hears in Revelation 6:9-11. I am not certain just when this fifth seal is opened, but it must be late in the first half of the Tribulation. It is evident, however, that the slaughter of the church has not yet ended. The number of fellow servants and brothers who were to be killed, as they had been, was not yet completed. In chapter seven we will be at the end of the first half of the Tribulation and their number is completed -- a multitude that no one could count.

Revelation 6:12-17
The Sixth Seal
The Great Earthquake

Read carefully the following passage of Scripture concerning what will happen when the sixth seal is opened. Whatever John is describing in these verses, it is evident that something catastrophic has occurred:

There was a great earthquake. The sun became black as sackcloth. The moon became as blood. The stars of heaven fell unto earth. The heavens departed as a scroll. Every mountain and island was moved. Men everywhere hid themselves in caves. They cried to the rocks to fall on them to hide them from the wrath of the Lamb.

This is no mere earthquake. This sounds more like a description of a nuclear war. It is certainly a powerful detonation of tremendous energy such as mankind has never experienced.

Just when does this occur? If we follow the

chronology of the chart we can pinpoint this cataclysmic event precisely at the close of the first three and a half years of the Great Tribulation.

We don't have a newspaper describing the events that led up to this nuclear confrontation, but we do have the Bible and a detailed account of what is going to happen in the Middle East to trigger this nuclear confrontation. That account is not in the Book of Revelation. The prophet Ezekiel wrote about it hundreds of years earlier. We read about it in the Book of Ezekiel chapters 38 and 39. There in the Old Testament Ezekiel prophecies a significant development in world affairs that will occur 2500 years after he wrote about it. We will see that prophecy take place midpoint in the Tribulation.

When Antichrist first came into power as president of the European Economic Community, the world was enjoying relative peace and prosperity. That peace had come through a covenant he made with Israel. The Jewish nation would be defended and protected by the European Economic Community. As a condition of peace between Israel and the Arabs, Israel agreed to disarm. Both Jews and Arabs will do away with all their aircraft, missiles, tanks and other armament. Ezekiel describes in chapter thirty eight how Israel was to live in peace and safety (38:8) in unwalled cities with no protection. A powerful nation from the North, called Gog and Magog by the prophet, moves into Palestine, probably for the great oil and mineral wealth in Israel. There is little doubt in the minds of most Bible Scholars that the prophet is referring to Russia, the "bear" from the North. Ezekiel tells us that it is not only Russia who invades Israel, but also her many satellite nations. Do not be too hasty in dismissing Russia from Bible prophecy because of the collapse of the former Soviet Union. God's word is not fickle. World events do not alter Bible prophecy. There will be a nuclear confrontation between East and West.

This will not be the battle of Armageddon. That battle will take place three and a half years later at the end of the seven years of Tribulation. From reading Ezekiel it appears that midpoint in the Tribulation the armies of Russia will march through Israel on their way to conquer and plunder Egypt. When this army returns to Palestine they are confronted by the forces of the United Community of Europe and her allies, and a short but devastating war ensues. Ezekiel describes the carnage in Israel, John describes the destruction of Russia by the detonation of the first nuclear weapons used in war since Nagasaki and Hiroshima.

John was there and tells us what he saw. "There was a great earthquake. The sun turned black like sackcloth made of goats hair. The moon turned blood red. The stars in the sky fell to earth." John is probably describing a multiple nuclear warhead detonated from space. "The sky receded like a scroll and every mountain and island was moved from its place."

Although what John describes is very graphic, it is very concise. You and I who live in the twentieth century can imagine what devastation would result from such a nuclear confrontation between two world powers. Two vast nations will virtually be destroyed. The entire planet will reel under the impact of nuclear warheads so powerful that even the islands isolated in the middle of the oceans will feel the tremor. These seismic repercussions result from nuclear explosions detonated over such cities as Moscow, Kiev, Lenningrad, Washington, Los Angeles and Chicago. It is no wonder that powerful, brave, mighty men will hide in caves and cry for the rocks to fall on them to hide them from the wrath of God. The war will not last long, but it will be far more devastating than you and I could ever imagine. That one nuclear engagement will bring to a close the first half of the Tribulation period. This is not the end by any means. It is the end of God's mercy and grace.

Before we get into our study of the second half of the Tribulation with the plagues of the trumpets and bowls, we will first return to the Rapture and see what John tells us about the church on earth during those tribulation years. He begins that story in chapter twelve. This is the beginning of Division Four covering The Tribulation Church. It parallels the action of Division Three -- The Saints Organized in Heaven.

The fact that there are parallel chapters in the Book of Revelation is one of the most significant discoveries I have made in the years I have devoted to the study of the Book of Revelation. As I said earlier, John does not write the Book of Revelation chronologically. He tells the story of the church from the Rapture to the Second Coming and then in chapter twelve goes back to the Rapture to tell us again about the church, but this time it is the Tribulation Church on Earth. So we are going to pause midpoint in the Tribulation and go back to the Rapture, the beginning of the story.

What we are doing in this study is not a violation of the principles of hermaneutics or Bible interpretation. Let me illustrate what I mean. Note that Genesis chapter one is the story of creation. Then in chapter two the creation story is repeated with other details and from a different perspective. The two Books of Chronicles are another example.They tell the same historical events related in the books of Samuel and Kings. Many people who have read the Bible for years believe that the Old Testament begins with Genesis and ends with Malichi, when in fact the history of the Old Testament concludes with the Book of Esther. The remaining twenty two books had all been written before the account of Queen Esther and can only be properly understood when each book -- the Psalms of Moses and David, the prophesies of Isaiah and Daniel, for example, are related to their proper chronology in the historical record. King Uzziah of Isaiah chapter six is the same Uzziah of Hosea 1:1 and I Chronicles 6:24 and II Chronicles 26:12-23. Our discovery that these passages of the Old Testament are not written in chronological order clarifies a lot of confusion in understanding them. A similar discovery as to how John wrote enlightens the Book of Revelation. You will see when we study these parallel passages (Divisions Three, Four and Five) that each section contributes a great deal to the clarification of the other. Treated separately they seem to elude any logical interpretation.

This explains why we leave the story in Revelation chapter six and pick it up in chapter twelve. In chapter twelve John goes back to the Rapture and relates what has been happening on earth during the breaking of the first six seals.

THE BRIGHT SIDE OF THE APOCALYPSE

REVELATION CHAPTER TWELVE

DIVISION FOUR

**The Rapture
Satan turns his attack
towards the repentant
Church on earth**

Chapters 12 – 16

Revelation 12:1-5
The Church Caught up in the
Rapture to the Throne of God

Never forget that the Book of Revelation is a study of the church. In the chapters we have already studied John has told us of the church caught up in the Rapture and gathered around the throne. He told us about the saints organized in heaven to evangelize and administer judgment here on earth during the first half of the Tribulation. In chapter twelve John is on earth where he will watch the church snatched away to meet the Lord in the air. He will remain on earth for the next three and a half years and will relate the story of the Tribulation Church.

In this passage there are three principle symbols we must identify. Once we have made that identification, the interpretation of the passage will be obvious. The three symbols are (1) the woman clothed with the sun (2) the child that is about to be born (3) and the great dragon.

First we will consider who the woman is. Most Bible teachers err in assuming that the woman represents the Jewish nation. They conclude that the child about to be born is Jesus Christ. Such an interpretation takes chapter twelve totally out of the context of the Book of Revelation and chooses to retell the story of the Jews. The Book of Revelation is not the story of the Jews. It is the story of the church.

The woman clothed with the sun is the church. Jesus said of the church, "Ye are the light of the world." The fact that she has the moon under foot refers to her dominion over the works of darkness. The crown of twelve stars represents the twelve apostles. The woman represents the visible church made up of countless denomin- ations worldwide. She is in fact all the churches from Ephesus to Laodicea. Even the worldly lukewarm congregation where Jesus stands outside the door knocking, seeking entrance, is called the church.

Within the church there are all classes of people -- good and bad, believers and hypocrites. Some are worldly and far from Christian. There is no doubt that there are many tares sown among the wheat just as Jesus said it would be. The church represented symbolically by the woman is the visible church made up of many denominations and independent congregations.

The invisible church, represented by the child who is about to be born, is within the visible church. These are the true believers, the born again. Those who believe on Jesus Christ as Lord and Saviour are represented by the child about to be separated from his mother's womb. They will be caught up to heaven in the Rapture.

There are a couple of analogies in Scriptures that verify what I am saying. The coming of Christ, the Rapture of the church, the redemption of our bodies are all referred to by Paul in Romans eight and by Christ in Matthew twenty-four. In each case the analogy is of a woman in travail of birth.

For we know that the whole creation groaneth and travaileth together in pain until now. And not only they, but ourselves also which have the first fruits of the Spirit even we ourselves

groan within ourselves awaiting for the adoption, to wit, the redemption of our body.
Romans 8:22, 23

Jesus used the same figure of speech in the Mount of Olives discourse, when He referred to His coming in the Rapture.

All these things are the beginning of sorrows.
Matthew 24:8

The expression "the beginning of sorrows" could better be translated "the beginnings of birthpains."

Already the church is experiencing the beginnings of birthpains in anticipation of the day when the invisible church (the true church) will be separated from the visible church and caught up to the throne of God. Although the church has anticipated the return of Christ for many centuries I doubt that there was ever a greater sense of expectancy within the true body of believers. A man and his wife, looking forward for nine months towards the birth of their first child, have a special awareness as the due date gets closer and closer. That is particularly true when they begin to count the intervals between labor pains. These birthpains are the special signs that it is time to be ready. It won't be long. Christ and the

Apostles gave us many signs that foretell the imminent return of Christ. Just as with the birth-pains, those signs are appearing closer and closer together. "When you see these things coming to pass, look up, your redemption draweth nigh."

Paul referred to the Rapture as "the day of the redemption of our bodies." At the Rapture we will all be changed. This mortal will put on immortality. We will experience the redemption of our bodies. This old sickly body of mine isn't simply going to get better. It will be totally changed. The new body will look like me. It will be me. But there will be many changes. For example, I will no longer be bald and paunchy and will have no need to wear glasses. At the Rapture an instantaneous change will take place in each of our bodies. It will be like a new birth. Christ will give us a new body. John is telling us here that the child is about to be born.

We have identified two of the symbols. There is no question as to who is the third. He is the "great red dragon." John very clearly identifies him in chapter twelve verse nine "...the great dragon was cast out, that old serpent called the Devil and Satan." His seven heads and ten horns and the seven crowns on his heads associate Satan with the kingdom of Antichrist.

Now that we have the three characters

identified, we want to look at the action, at what is happening. In Revelation 12:2 the day approaches when the woman, the visible church, is about to give birth to the child. I am part of that visible Church. You probably are too. I am a member of one denomination; you may be a member of another. I am Protestant; you may be Catholic. I am also part of the invisible church, that group of people within all denominations who are the true born again believers. The day when the two will be separated cannot be far off. There are no unfulfilled prophecies that could impede the Rapture. There is no reason Christ could not return for His church today.

In verse three the third character of this drama enters the scene. It is Satan, the mighty dragon. He knows that the Rapture will seal his doom. He will do everything within his power to block the Rapture of the church and will make every effort to "devour the child as soon as it is born."

The problem is that he does not know when the child will be born. That is the most guarded secret of the universe. Jesus told His disciples while He was here on earth that He himself did not know at what hour the Son of Man would return. If Christ did not know, you can be certain Satan does not know. It will be a secret and sudden Rapture that will catch even the devil, the dragon, by surprise. We will, be snatched away from his clutches.

In the meantime Satan has devoted his principle efforts for these past two thousand years to cause every believer to give up, to fall by the wayside, and miss the Rapture. He doesn't want you and me to be ready. Paul said that Satan "goes about seeking whom he may devour." He is tempting, attacking, tormenting the saints everywhere to cause us to fall into sin, to succumb, to miss that glorious day. Satan is aware that if I sin I can confess that sin and be forgiven and restored. He is also aware of something that many Christians and even ministers of the Gospel overlook. That is there will be no time to confess my sin and repent when the trumpet sounds. I will be ready or left behind. It would be the Devil's satanic delight to succeed in seducing thousands upon thousands of Christians as he did the pastor in our parable. That is what Revelation 12:4 is telling us. Satan wants to devour us in the very moment of the Rapture. He doesn't want us to be ready. What a victory for him. How sad for the Christian who had walked faithfully with the Lord for years, but missed it like the five foolish virgins who weren't ready.

Those believers who were ready at Christ's

coming are snatched away from Satan's clutches. They are safe in heaven with the Lord. That is the event described by Paul, in his first letter to the Thessalonians.

And the dead in Christ shall rise first then we which are alive and remain shall be caught up together with them in the clouds; to meet the Lord in the air; so shall we ever be with the Lord.

I Thessalonians 4:16,17

John proceeds to tell us what will happen next

Revelation 12:6-12
Satan Battles With Michael the Archangel
Trying to Block the Rapture

Read this passage carefully. You will note that there are two different battles described. The war in heaven, discussed in 12:7-9, is not the same incident of Satan cast out of heaven in 12:3 and 4. The first battle took place before the creation of man, possibly millions of years ago. The second battle will take place at the Rapture. Satan knows that he will have but seven years between the Rapture and the Second Coming, and then will come his final judgment. That is why the Word says in 12:12 "He knows that his time is short."

The one who is called the accuser of the brethren will be terribly agitated the day the believers are caught up to heaven. He will challenge the right of every one of us to enter heaven. "These are sinners. They have lied. They have cheated. They have no right to enter heaven." He accuses us of having committed all manner of sins, and his accusations are true. For all of us have sinned. All are doomed to hell. We have no right to God's forgiveness. Satan insists that we deserve to suffer the same fate as he and his angels who will burn eternally in the lake of fire. Yes, we are sinners, but sinners saved by grace. We are sinners who have been forgiven and who have been washed clean by the blood of the Lamb. We are overcomers. Christ will welcome us home, and will cast Satan, the red dragon, down to earth. The resurrection and the Rapture will take place.

Paul speaks a great deal in his writings of the power of the resurrection. The most powerful demonstration of God's omnipotence since the creation of the universe will be the Rapture of the living church and the resurrection of the dead in Christ. Should the Rapture take place right now before I finish writing this sentence, my godly mother who died many years ago and is buried on a hillside in Western Pennsylvania, will rise from the dead and join me here on the west coast. Angels will escort us into the glory John described in chapter four. How can that be? My mother is dead for more than thirty years. What would remain of her body if it were exhumed today? Probably nothing. The resurrection seems to be incredible, if not impossible.

The Bible compares the resurrection to a kernel of corn planted in the ground. The kernel apparently dies and rots away. Out of that decay a plant grows. It has nothing in common with the corn that was planted. The green plant that sprouts from the kernel is different. The plant has leaves. It has roots. The kernel of corn had nothing like that. A stalk of corn in no way resembles a kernel of corn. Yet, when that stalk produces, the fruit will be an ear of corn with kernels identical to that which was planted. If I could understand the miracle of how that happens in my garden, I might better understand the resurrection. Paul explained it to the Corinthians.

But someone may ask, How can the dead be raised? With what kind of a body will they come? How foolish. What you sow does not come to life unless it dies. When you sow you do not plant the body that will be, but just a seed, perhaps of wheat or something else. But

God gives it a body as He determined. And to each kind of seed he gives its own body . . . so it will be in the resurrection of the dead. The body that is sown is perishable It is sown in dishonor, it is raised in power.It is sown a natural body, it is raised a spiritual body. If there is a natural body, there is also a spiritual body.

II Corinthians 15:35-38

The first words we will hear when we arrive in heaven will be, "Now is salvation come." (Rev 12:10) We need to clarify the meaning of this word "salvation". We say we are saved right now, but in reality we are on probation. The term used throughout the New Testament is not "those who are saved" but rather "those who are being saved." None of us will be saved until we have reached our heavenly home. It is much like being on a ship that sinks at sea hundreds of miles from shore and leaves us floundering in the ocean crying out to be rescued. A lifeboat comes by and we are pulled from a watery grave. We could say that we are saved, yet we are hundreds of miles from the safety of shore and home.

None of us will be saved until we reach home. Can you sense the elation you and I will feel on that day when we are finally out of Satan's reach? There will be no more trials, no more temptations, no more failure. I cannot imagine the overwhelming peace we will know when we hear those words, "Enter thou into the joy of the Lord." No joy you have ever experienced will be comparable to the bliss and elation of that glorious day. This is certainly the brightest side of the apocalypse.

But after the Rapture what will it be like in the world we left behind? John is about to tell us in the next few verses.

Revelation 12:13-17
Satan Turns His Attack
Towards the Repentant Church on Earth

Certainly such an event as the coming of Christ in the Rapture will be newsworthy. Hundreds of thousands of people will disappear without a plausible explanation. But then again, the impact may not be as great as you and I might think. There are many communities throughout the world where there are no Christians, and many more communities where the Rapture will take only two or three or a half dozen believers. Consider the probabilities in the United States, a supposedly Christian nation. A city with a population of 100,000 could have as many as 500 or 1000 born again Christians who will be missing on that day. Ninety percent of the inhabitants of that city, however, will not know any of those Christians because they don't live in the same social circle. The Christians around you who leave will not even be missed by thousands of people who live in your community.   If you are here after the Rapture you will read about it in the papers and there will be many explanations given as to what happened.

There might be a few accidents when driverless cars careen off the street or highway and the police report will state that the driver fled the scene of the accident.

The classes at the university will convene as usual even though a few students will be absent without excuse. Who will miss them?

A husband will come home from work and will discover that his wife and child are missing. He will probably tell the neighbors that she went to visit her mother. Or he will invent some other logical reason to explain their absence. He certainly will not say, "The Lord came and took them."

There could very well be tremendous havoc and disaster with great loss of life the day the Rapture takes place. I can imagine the death resulting from driverless cars, and planes without pilots plunging to disaster. When Jesus talked to his disciples about how it would be at the Rapture, he told them in Luke

I tell you, in that night there shall be two in one bed, the one shall, be taken and the other left. Two women shall be grinding together, the one shall be taken and the other left. Two men shall, be in the field, the one shall be taken and the other left

Luke 17:34-36

Then the disciples raised the question of "Where, Lord," and Jesus answered them in a very peculiar way.

Withersoever the body is, thither will the eagles be gathered together.

Luke 17:37

Could Jesus be referring to the vultures gathered over the dead bodies scattered across the earth as the inevitable result of accidents caused by the saints being caught up to heaven?

For a day or two the newspapers will play up the disappearance of hundreds of thousands of people throughout the world. Many explanations will be given. Some will say they were kidnapped by terrorists. The media will account for their absence by a variety of plausible explanations. Some science fiction oriented reporters will attribute their disappearance to extra terrestrial aliens in flying saucers. Science will give some logical explanation such as a mysterious attraction from a passing star that somehow sucked them all into outer space.

If all 350 people of the congregation where I attend church left some Sunday morning for a mountain retreat without telling anybody, who would miss them? At the Rapture many people will think those religious kooks have gone off someplace to do their weird thing.

As spectacular as these headlines might be, within a few days other matters will take preeminence in the news and the phenomenon of the Rapture will be forgotten. It will be similar to what happened one Sunday afternoon in Peru, South America when an earthquake shook the region of Callejon de Huallas causing the death and disappearance of nearly 100,000 people. The event was news for one day. The world soon forgot that tragedy. So it will be at the Rapture.

Many of you who are reading these pages right now will be alive and on earth after the Rapture. If you are, I hope that the reality of what I am writing will give you an understanding of what has happened, and what to expect, and how to react. Let me tell you now, find a Bible and hide it in a safe secure place. It will be your cherished possession. You can be certain that the authorities will make every effort to destroy every Bible in existence.

"Why", you may ask," do you assume that I might be left behind? I am a Christian. I believe in Jesus Christ. I belong to the church and I am a good person." I don't want to offend anyone, but many of you who think you are ready to go will be left behind. Not all those who say, "Lord, Lord," will enter. Jesus said that there will be those who had preached in Christ's name, who had cast out demons and had healed the sick in His name -- yet He will say, "Depart I know ye not". I don't believe Jesus was talking about hypocritical charlatans who are set on deceiving the public. He was talking about people who actually think that they are ready. There will be millions of disappointed church members left on earth to go through the Tribulation. If you are one of those left after the Rapture, there will still be hope. Let me tell you what you should do.

If I were that pastor in our parable who was left behind because of a moment's gratification of fleshly lust, I would fall on my knees, repent of my sins and find a place of forgiveness. Let me assure you that it will be possible for you to repent and be saved after the Rapture.

The thought that comes to many people is that this amounts to a "second chance" after they have missed it. In a sense that is true, but it is not in violation of any principle of Scripture. I am not talking of a second chance after death. When Christ comes in the air and raptures the church, life on earth will go on as always. You will live in the same house. You will go to work at the same job. This is not a second chance after death. The most natural thing for you to do, if you are here after the church had been taken, will be to repent and to seek forgiveness of God. This is especially true if you have knowledge of God's Word and recognize that what happened was the Rapture, and you missed it.

Let's go back to John's writings to see what life will be like for you on earth during the Tribulation. I assume you will consider siding with the believers and will become a part of the Tribulation Church. I can tell you this. It will not be easy to be a Christian during the Tribulation. It will be extremely difficult to live a Christian life. The truth is every Christian you become acquainted with will be martyred. If you think living the Christian life now is difficult, don't count on waiting to accept Christ during the Tribulation.

In chapter twelve, verse six, John wrote of the woman whom I identified as the church remaining on earth. Two dramatic changes will take place before she flees into the wilderness. The Tribulation church will not be the same as the church in verse one, pictured as the woman waiting to deliver her child.

The first change is that the child, the true church, was taken away and caught up to heaven. Every born again believer who was ready at that instant left. The majority of congregations will be without pastors. The church after the Rapture will not be made up of a worshipping community of believers. The church will be a frightened, confused assembly of worldly, luke-warm members who probably will accept that the Rapture has taken place, and they will be scared.

A second change will occur. The church that Jesus Christ will recognize on earth during the Tribulation will be exclusively the repentant believers who will make their confession of Christ and will find an experience of spiritual restoration. The church will be purged of all hypocrisy. Millions who now call themselves church members will disassociate themselves from the body of believers after the Rapture. That will be the "great falling away" Paul talked about in II Thessalonians 2:13.

Let no man deceive you by any means, for that day shall not come except there come a falling away first, and that man of sin be revealed, the son of perdition.

II Thessalonians 2:3

When Paul speaks of "the day" he refers to the Second Coming and not the Rapture. The "falling away" and the "revealing of Antichrist" both come after the Rapture and in the order that Paul gives us -- first the falling away, and then the appearance of Antichrist. We are living in the last days before the Rapture, but we are not seeing a falling away. The church is experiencing revival around the world. Thousands upon thousands are being brought into the kingdom of Christ every day.A greater percentage of the general population is in church every week now than in any other period of church history. The falling away comes after the Rapture and is a result of the millions of lukewarm church members abandoning their hypocritical empty practice of religion. The core that is left is the church which will go through the first three and a half years of Tribulation. They will be as much the body of Christ as those who were taken up in the Rapture. Jesus spoke of these believers in Matthew twenty-four and told us of the horrendous tribulation that they will go through and concluded his discussion with these somber words -- "He that endures to the end shall be saved."

That effort of endurance begins right away. Immediately after the Rapture the believers will be scattered. There will be no meetings in beautiful, churches, seated on cushioned pews, enjoying choral music and eloquent sermons. The believers will flee, leaving their unbelieving spouses and children if necessary. It will be a struggle for survival against a godless state. Verse six says that they flee into the wilderness

And the woman fled into the wilderness where she hath a place prepared of God, that they should feed her there a thousand two hundred and threescore days.

Revelation 12:6

That wilderness may or may not be a place. I am aware that the verse says that it was a place that God prepared for them. I don't believe, however, that this verse is saying that all the Christians of the world will be concentrated in one central location. It could mean that every individual believer will have a special place prepared for him. You can be sure that God will take care of that church. Who do you suppose the "they" are of 12:6 who will be given the assignment of caring for this fleeing church? We already saw in our study of chapter six the saints in heaven organized and sent back to earth to feed the church during those critical three and a half years. They are represented by the rider on the black horse of Revelation chapter six. These saints will be sent back to earth to administer the rationing of food during the inevitable famine. They are the saints referred to in Revelation 12:6. The Christians will suffer much pain and misery during the Tribulation. Yet, the joy of the Lord will be their strength just as it is today. If you turn to Christ after the Rapture you will not be alone. Many people where you live will repent and be saved. Besides these new believers, you will undoubtedly meet some of those immortal saints from heaven who will be placed in strategic locations. They will be a great encouragement to you and other mortal Christians on earth. You will be aware of God's promise to "never leave you nor forsake you." You will not be alone. In the midst of the darkness there will be a bright side of the apocalypse.

And when the dragon saw that he was cast unto earth, he persecuted the woman which brought forth the man child. And to the woman were given two wings of a great eagle that she might fly into the wilderness, unto her place, where she is nourished for a time, and times and a half time from the face of the

serpent. And the serpent cast out of his mouth water as a flood after the woman, that he might cause her to be carried away of the flood. And the earth helped the woman, and the earth opened her mouth and swallowed up the flood which the dragon cast out of his mouth.

Revelation 12:13-16

Satan will be defeated in his effort to block the raptured church from entering heaven and will be cast down to earth. The devil knows that his time will be short. He will have only seven years before the Second Coming of Christ and the final judgment. He will try desperately to get back at God, but he cannot reach Him. He can only touch God by relentless attacks on God's children. This has been Satan's tactic since the Garden of Eden. His purpose has always been to deceive and destroy us. His lures of exotic and erotic enticements are not to bring us pleasure, but to damn our soul. The devil is not our friend. He wants us in his power, under his heel. His plan is that you and I will occupy hell that was prepared for him and his fallen angels.

Satan will realize that he missed his chance to damn the invisible church caught up to heaven.

They are forever safe from satan's attacks. However, he will soon be aware that a new church has formed on earth, those who had faith enough to believe in God for forgiveness even though they had missed the Rapture. Satan will turn his attention to those believers.

It is Satan himself who directs this persecution in chapter twelve We know from Revelation 13:5 that Antichrist will be in power for forty-two months or three and a half years. We also know that he is still in power at the time of the fifth plague which is the plague of the trumpet/bowls. That will come late in the second half of the Tribulation. Evidently the rise of the antichrist will not occur until a year or so after the Rapture. The antichrist is not on the scene here in chapter twelve. It is the devil who makes a concerted effort to stamp out the fledgling church that will once again spring up on earth.

In verse seventeen John introduces another element in this conflict "...the remnant of her seed." Look carefully at that verse, Revelation 12:17, and you will see that Satan is engaged in the pursuit of not only the Christians who missed the Rapture, but their offspring as well. "Those who obey God's commandments and hold to the testimony of Jesus." Who are these? They wlll not be the physical natural children of the Christians, but their spiritual offspring. Those new Christians will make up the bulk of the vast multitude who eventually will be saved out of the Tribulation. Although Satan will become aware of a few thousand restored believers on earth, he will not expect them to survive, much less grow in number. Obviously there would be no way the Tribulation Church could flourish, but they will. God's plan to support those believers will give them the enabling grace to add millions to their numbers during the first forty-two months of the Tribulation.

In chapter twelve we see that plan unfold. Of course it will not be very evident to the world what is happening. If you are left on earth and have enough presence of mind and spiritual insight to recognize that you need God in your life, you will probably contact those Christians and you will begin to sense the power of their faith that gives them strength and assurance.I can imagine that it will be a troublesome time for you. You have been a good person. You may even want to defend the Christians. But when you see the appalling treatment that they are receiving you will question why anyone would want to become a believer under such circumstances. It will be easier for you to comply with society, conform to the world and enjoy the prosperity of the new world order. It will be hard to say, "I want to be a Christian too."

After the believers are caught up in the Rapture the attitude of the world will be "Good riddance." That bunch of fanatics will not be here to spoil their fun. The world will think they are rid of them. The fact is a brand new church will spring up, more dynamic and more powerful than ever. The ACLU, the atheists, the New Agers, and all those other godless groups who have been trying to impede the ministry of the church before the Rapture will be enraged that the church will still be alive and well on earth.

The new church will not seem to be much of a threat at first. Since the vast majority of pastors, Bible teachers and missionaries will have left in the Rapture, the church will be virtually without leadership. Small groups of believers will begin to meet in secret much as the early Christians did in the catacombs of Rome. It will be a miracle that such a decimated organization survives in the face of the horrendous persecution that will confront them.

When Satan incites the world to turn against the believers, the persecution will not be as it is today. The Christian will have no legal rights. Those who are set on stamping out the church will forego any niceties. There will be no law against killing Christians. The reality will be that those who believe in Christ will be sought out and killed without mercy and their bullet ridden bodies will be left lying on the streets and sidewalks of your community.

Years ago I lived in Chile, South America when General Pinochet overthrew the communist regime. The new government enforced a curfew prohibiting anyone but the military to be on the streets of any city or town between the hours of 10:00 p.m. and 5:00 a.m. Anyone who violated that curfew was summarily executed and his body left lying where he was shot for all to see the next day. I have seen such corpses lying on the sidewalk in pools of blood. It is a grim reminder not to violate the curfew. Let me tell you, the sight of those dead bodies was an effective deterrent. Any of those who accept Christ after the Rapture are going to suffer a similar fate. It doesn't look as if there is a very bright side to the apocalypse for that hated segment of society called the church. Why would anyone want to throw in their lot with that band of Christians? It doesn't look as if the church of Christ could survive in such a godless demonic society.

Satan will expect to wipe this crowd off the face of the Earth. He will bring against the believers a flood of opposition described in 12:15. The figure of speech used by John to describe how

Satan will attack the church is, "The dragon cast out water from his mouth so as to sweep her away in the flood." As in other passages in Revelation, the metaphor "water" represents the people of many nations. Evidently Satan will turn the heathen population against the church. The carnage will be gruesome. Anyone who professes the name of Christ will be marked to be killed. There will be no escape. Even at home believers will be attacked by members of their own family who will turn against them and report them to the authorities. It will be a sad day for the families in which some members are believers and others are not. Husbands will turn against their spouses and children against their parents. Children in school will be trained to betray their own loved ones. Families will be torn apart. I am sure that there will be much pressure on neighbors to report any religious activities they might observe. In chapter six of Revelation we read that peace will be taken from the earth and many will die by the sword. Undoubtedly the fear and despair from that bloodshed will be overwhelming. In that desperate situation we come to the exciting part of the story. Revelation 12:16 tells us how the church manages to survive the attacks of Satan. God will raise up an invincible army that will completely swallow up the flood. These will be saints organized in heaven and sent back to earth in their immortal spiritual bodies to defend the church and extend its influence to the ends of the earth.

Now I can understand how those helpless, disoriented, leaderless, decimated believers will manage not only to survive, but to conquer. If you are here and have any association with the Christians, you will eventually come across some of those evangelists who will be winning converts to the cause of Christ. These will be the "sent ones" of chapter six. These extraordinary evangelists will be unlike any men or women you have ever met. When you meet one it will be your first contact with an immortal being living in a spiritual resurrected body. That body itself will be incredible and capable of doing fantastic things. What fear would you have of the death squads of Satan after talking to one of these from the other side? This is why millions will accept Christ in the face of certain martyrdom.

Not only will these evangelists win countless numbers to Christ, they will be a great source of encouragement to you as a renewed Christian. These men and women will be a tremendous boost to your faith. They will have reached the other side. They will have passed through the portals of heaven. They will have seen Jesus Christ face to face. They will have tasted the unsearchable riches of the glory of Christ. They will certainly urge you to hang in there. You will then see God's plan unfolding. You will understand the prophecies of Revelation. You will see the works of Satan and Antichrist in a different light. You will see what God's plan is for this world as He takes it from the possession and control of Satan and restores our planet Earth to the beauty of its original creation. Even though it will cost you a great deal of suffering and eventually your life to accept Jesus Christ as your Saviour, it will be worth it all.

This is not fiction. This is not the wild imagination of some fanatic. This is a sane interpretation of what John wrote. When we see the participation of the immortal saints in the story of the Tribulation Church that body of believers stands out in a totally different light. It will not be all dark. Satan will not be in control. There will be a bright side to the apocalypse -- a glorious bright side that so many have missed in their study of this fantastic book.

THE BRIGHT SIDE OF THE APOCALYPSE

LESSON VIII

DIVISION FOUR

The Tribulation Church
The rise of Antichrist
The rise of the False
Prophet

Chapters 12 – 16

REVELATION CHAPTER THIRTEEN

Revelation 13:1-10
The Rise of Antichrist

Chapter thirteen introduces the man called Antichrist or the "beast out of the sea." This is the "man of sin" or the "son of perdition" referred to by Paul in II Thessalonians chapter two.

Let no man deceive you by any means. For that day shall not come except there come a falling away first and that man of sin be revealed, the son of perdition.   II Thess. 2:3

When Paul wrote in this passage about the coming of the Lord Jesus Christ he was not referring to the Rapture but to the Second Coming. Two things will occur after the Rapture. First, millions of lukewarm hypocritical church members will disassociate themselves from the body of believers. That is the falling away. Then Antichrist will appear on the scene, but not until several months later.

Antichrist has several different names in the Bible. Isaiah 14:4 calls him the King of Babylon. Daniel calls him "the little horn" in Daniel 7:8 and 8:9. The ten horns seen by Daniel represent the ten nations that will make up the core of the revived Roman empire. According to Daniel seven of the nations will submit willingly to the rule of Antichrist while three will be forced into submission. One political figure will emerge from those ten European nations and become the world leader. John calls him "a beast that comes out of the sea." -- the sea of humanity. The symbol of the sea is explained in Revelation 17:15 "The waters you saw are people, multitudes, nations, languages." What John wanted to clarify was that Antichrist will not be the devil, nor a demon spirit, but a mere man as normal and human as any other man. Although John calls him a beast, that does not describe what

Antichrist will look like. He was describing his nature, his cruelty, his ferocity. So when John described him as a beast that resembled a leopard with feet of a bear and a mouth of a lion we are aware that this has nothing to do with his physical appearance. Rather, John was referring to his character, personality and actions.

In reality, Antichrist will be a very attractive and personable individual. He will win the admiration and allegiance of the entire world. He will have an irresistible charisma and magnetism that will carry him to world leadership. Satan will enable him to achieve that powerful position and will give to Antichrist special occult powers enabling him to deceive the people. With these powers he will counterfeit the miracles of Christ with many signs and wonders. His ultimate performance of deceit will be to die from a mortal wound and revive. It is interesting the way John expressed it -- "He seemed to have a fatal wound." Revelation 13:3 Antichrist will be a clever deceiver and he will certainly convince the world that he has risen from the dead.

The philosophy of Antichrist is humanism which says that man has no need for Jesus Christ, the Bible, or His church. We are quite capable of solving our own problems. This is the basic philosophy of education in our school system and government today. Our minds are being saturated with humanistic philosophy. It is all in preparation for the coming Antichrist. The practice of the occult and the preeminence of astrology are both signs of Satan's preparation of the world for the acceptance and acclaim of Antichrist as a world leader. The signs are so real and evident. It is almost frightening to think of how close we must be living to those very scenes depicted in the Book of Revelation.

John clearly stated in Revelation 13:5 that Antichrist will exercise his authority for forty-two months -- three and a half years. Probably his rule will begin a year or so into the Tribulation, and not immediately after the Rapture. We know this because we will find the "beast" Antichrist in power at the time the sixth bowl is poured out in chapter sixteen. That happens near the close of the second half of the seven years of Tribulation.

Revelation 13:11-18
The Rise of the False Prophet

Revelation chapter thirteen introduces another beast. That beast is the false prophet, the leader of the world church, whose headquarters will be in Rome, the modern Babylon.

Revelation 13:4 says that this world church

leader will have two horns, symbolic of two political heads of power. The two horns of the false prophet are symbolic of the two religious kingdoms that will come together to form his satanic church. Those two religious bodies in my opinion will be (1) the World Council of Churches and (2) the Roman Catholic Church.

To identify the World Council of Churches and the Roman Catholic Church as the base of the church of the false prophet is not a slur against those religious organizations. Remember, the Christians within those two groups will go to heaven in the Rapture. Only a shell of those organizations will be left on earth to go through the Tribulation. During that time the people who make up those two bodies will be those who were not ready to meet the Lord. If the Pope of Rome has accepted Jesus Christ as his personal Saviour and if he is living a victorious Spirit filled life he will be caught up in the Rapture with the rest of us. If not, he will be left behind like every other person who failed to make the necessary preparations to be ready for the Master's return. No one knows who will emerge as the head of the false church of the Tribulation.

This false prophet, like Antichrist, will receive his power and direction from Satan, the red dragon. Antichrist is the beast that comes out of the sea (humanity). The second beast, the false prophet, will come out of the earth. This is the beast who will kill the two witnesses in chapter eleven and there he is identified in verse seven as the beast out of the abyss, the abode of the fallen angels. This means that this church leader will not be an ordinary human being. He is not a demon possessed man like Antichrist. There will be three personalities who will form a satanic trinity. Satan himself takes the place of God. Antichrist is Satan incarnate in the flesh and takes the place of Jesus Christ. The false prophet takes the place of the Holy Spirit.

The false prophet will receive his authority from the dragon, Satan. His role will be to promote the satanic worship of Antichrist. He is the one who will contrive the great image. It is not hard to decipher what that "great image" might be. I believe it will be a powerful computer capable of registering every person on the face of the earth. Every man, woman and child will be given an account number that will be permanently in-scribed invisibly in the palm of his right hand or in his forehead. There will be no need for cash or credit cards. When you make a purchase, a scanner will read the number on your hand. The computer will then deduct the appropriate amount from your bank account. This is not some hypothetical preposterous idea. Debit cards with that capability are already in use in many cities of the United States. A concerted effort is being made right now to bring all of our business and personal computers into compatibility with one great system. Those problems will soon be resolved, making this plan of the false prophet quite feasible. His plan has a devious aspect as well. Without the number inscribed on your hand or forehead you will not be able to buy or sell but to take the mark of the beast is to sell your soul to Satan and seal your eternal damnation.

The mission of the false prophet will be to destroy the church. His plan will be the "mark of the beast." The underlying purpose of this special mark will be to combat the rapidly growing Christian community. At first there will be only a few hundred thousand believers restored to grace after the Rapture, however, these will multiply to several millions under the impetus of world evangelism. Satan will use the mark of the beast to entrap those Christians.

It will be extremely difficult for the Christians. The relentless pursuit of the Christians by Antichrist and the false prophet will gradually expose the believers, and millions will suffer martyrdom. To accept Christ and live the Christian life during the Tribulation will not be easy. The believers will experience unspeakable suffering and ultimately, martyrdom.

Without the Lord's intervention, the forces of Satan would certainly prevail against God's kingdom on earth. But the Lord will intervene when he commissions hundreds of thousands of immortal saints to return to earth for their designated mission. You will meet some of these agents of the Lord if you are here on earth. They will have infiltrated every facet of commerce and government.They will have supernatural capabilities. They will be so perfectly desguised that the forces of Antichrist will not recognize them for who they are.   You will find these immortal saints infiltrated into every industry, every university, every hospital, every center of transportation and communication and in every branch of government. Their job will be to take peace from the earth.

This may sound like a chapter out of a James Bond thriller, but nothing that has been produced in the imagination of Hollywood can compare with what God plans to do through His people, the saints. Antichrist will be world leader of a sophisticated police state, yet with all his most modern weaponary he will be no match for the Lord and His people.

The next thing you can expect after this diabolical plan of the mark of the beast will be the beginnings of the famine. This was described in our study of chapter six when the rider of the black horse enters the scene. You will remember what we said. The rider of the black horse will not cause the famine. The famine will be a direct result of the activities of the saints represented by the rider on the fiery red horse.

The saints represented by the rider on the black horse will be sent to earth to administer, or at least control, a system of rationing. God's purpose again is to provide care and protection for His people. If you are a believer on earth at that time, you will be aware of the special treatment given the Christians by some of the officials in charge of rationing. The Lord will have His special people planted in these areas. These are the people referred to in 12:6. "**They** should feed her..." God has a plan to thwart the insidious scheme of Antichrist.

His foreordained plan will be accomplished. Everything will be on schedule. The Gospel will be preached. The body of believers will be built up. Millions will be brought into the kingdom That is why I can write about the bright side of the apocalypse.

Chapter thirteen describes the rise of Antichrist and the false prophet. It gives us some insight into their diabolical activities. The issues are spiritual. Antichrist will pit his power against Jesus Christ and His church. The Book of Revelation does not concern itself with the dynamics of world affairs. It does not tell us much about the rise and fall of world powers. A study of Ezekiel and Daniel would give us a greater understanding of those political interests. The principle and foremost concern of the Book of Revelation during the first three and a half years of the Tribulation is the building up of the body of Christ on earth. Not much is said about international affairs or about the activities of Antichrist, except as they pertain to the church. I cannot emphasize this point too much. This is the key to our understanding of the Book of Revelation. Early in our study we made it clear that the book does not concern itself with the Jews or the nations of the world, but exclusively deals with the church of Jesus Christ and the church's part in the eternal plan of God to expel Satan, his angels and his people from planet Earth.

The unveiling of that plan will be exciting. Every believer will be involved, whether you are one of those who is caught up in the Rapture or one of those on earth who found forgiveness and restoration after the Rapture. The work will be intense. Time will be short. The mission to be accomplished will be fantastic. The entire world will be evangelized in three and a half years. To those of you who are here on earth in mortal bodies suffering famine, fire, persecution, and pain it will seem like an eternity. But it will end. We know the precise length of that judgment mixed with grace -- 1260 days. At the end of those three and a half years of Tribulation the church will be taken up to heaven. That will occur midpoint in the seven years.

That is precisely where we are in our study, half way through the seven years. We have seen the first six seals broken. At the breaking of the sixth seal the world will experience its first nuclear war between two world powers. The period of evangelism will end and the Tribulation Church will be raptured.

That brings us to chapter seven in Division Three and chapter fourteen in Division Four.These two chapters describe identical events which occur midpoint in the seven year Tribulation. When we can see chapters seven and fourteen together and get them oriented as to their correct chronological place it is not difficult to interpret and understand their meaning. Most commentators that I have read do not seem to know when these scenes described by John occur and as a result their interpretation of these two chapters is anything but clear. When we put chapters seven and fourteen together in their correct sequence midpoint in the Tribulation, what John wrote is perfectly logical.

THE BRIGHT SIDE OF THE APOCALYPSE
LESSON IX

DIVISION THREE

144,000 converted Jews
sealed by Jesus Christ
The martyred Christians
welcomed home

Chapters 4-11

DIVISION FOUR

Harvest of martyred souls
The martyred Christians
welcomed home
The evangelists return
to heaven

Chapters 12 - 16

REVELATION
Chapters Seven and Fourteen

Chapters seven and fourteen are parallel chapters describing events midpoint in the Tribulation. These will occur three and a half years after the Rapture and three and a half years before the Second Coming. Let us review what has happened. After the opening of the sixth seal at the end of the first three and a half years the great armies of Russia marched on little unarmed Palestine. The European nations responded with nuclear weapons and a brief World War III ensued. It was brief because such a nuclear confrontation would be over in a matter of hours.

Although it was a devastating war, it is not the primary focus of John in Revelation. That is because this conflict had little, if anything, to do with the church. We can understand why when we see what happens in chapters seven and fourteen. Its mission accomplished, the Tribulation Church had already left before the nuclear confrontation explodes.

Revelation7:1
The 144,000 Converted Jews are
Sealed by Jesus Christ

There has been much speculation and many ridiculous claims as to who are these 144,000 people. They are exactly who John said they are, converted Jews. They are descendants of eleven of the twelve patriarchal tribes. This list does not include the tribe of Dan. That tribe will be replaced by the 12,000 representing the tribe of Manasses, one of the sons of Joseph.

The 144,000 are a small percentage of the millions of Jews who will be living in Palestine under the rule of Antichrist under a covenant treaty that Antichrist will make with the state of Israel. The terms of that treaty will restore the borders of Israel to conform to the pact God made with Abraham. Furthermore, that treaty will provide for the reconstruction of Solomon's temple on its original site in Jerusalem. In that temple the ancient ritual of animal sacrifices will be reinstated. Israel will again be a flourishing prosperous nation. Jews from around the world will migrate to their homeland and enjoy the peace, prosperity, and protection promised and provided by Antichrist.

Among the millions of Jews who migrate to Palestine there will be many thousands from each of the ten, so called, lost tribes of Israel. In reality these are not Jews, since the term "Jew" refers only to the descendent of Judah, the two southern kingdoms. The ten northern kingdoms were scattered across the face of the earth when Assyria overran their nation 500 years before the birth of Christ. No one today can identify those who belong to those ten lost tribes. However, God knows. He has no difficulty identifying them. God's intention is that those Jews return to their homeland, and He will arrange the circumstances that will bring them back to Palestine. God looks on with great satisfaction as ships and planes arrive at Haifa and Jerusalem bringing to the shores of Palestine millions of immigrant Jews rejoicing at their return to their ancient homeland.

Thousands of Jewish immigrants will respond to the witness of the Christian evangelists and accept Jesus Christ as their Messiah, Lord, and Saviour. That evangelism has continued three and a half years, and is about finished. "The hour of God's judgment is come." (Revelation 14:7) Before that judgment begins, two more spectacular events are to take place.

The first event concerns the 144,000.

Revelation 14:1-5
Jesus on Mount Sion with the 144,000
In a Worship Service

Here we see Jesus standing on Mount Sion, on earth, in Jerusalem with the 144,000 especially selected converted Jews. This cannot be the Second Coming of Christ as some would tell us. The event occurs in chapter 14 before the final plagues of the bowls, before the Battle of Armageddon, long before the return of Christ on a white horse in chapter nineteen. We can clarify the confusion when we put chapter fourteen and chapter seven together. Both chapters are describing events taking place midpoint in the Tribulation.

After a worship service, Jesus places a seal on the forehead of each of the 144,000. These have a very special destiny. They will be the church on earth during the second half of the Tribulation For three and a half years these Jewish converts will be the only Christians on the face of the earth. There is a reason why they are sealed.

I have often wondered what John meant when he said these 144,000 were "sealed of God." I think I now know. Those Jewish believers are called the "remnant" and the "first fruits." They will be the church, the only believers on earth when the Lord returns at the end of the Tribulation period. The seal is for their protection. Before these 144,000 are scattered across the face of the earth they are transformed from mortal to immortal beings. Jesus Christ gives them their spiritual bodies. You and I will receive ours when we are transformed at the Rapture.

However, these believers were never raptured. Neither are they included in the millions of martyrs caught up into heaven midpoint in the Tribulation. These Christian Jews will go through the Tribulation and will be on earth unscathed when Christ returns to usher in the millennium. I have often puzzled over the dilemma of explaining when these 144,000 would receive their immortal bodies. I now know. It will be here in chapter seven and fourteen when they receive the seal of God for their protection. That explains how it is that every one of these 144,000 converted Jews survives the terrible plagues that will buffet this planet Earth during the final three and a half years. Not one will be killed because they are immortal as you and I will be. Fantastic.

Jesus explains in Matthew 24:14-22 what John is describing in Revelation seven and fourteen.

And this Gospel of the kingdom shall be preached in all the world for a witness unto all nations and then shall the end come.

When ye therefore shall see the abomination of desolation spoken of by Daniel the prophet, stand in the holy place. (Whoso readeth let him understand.)Then let them which be in Judea flee into the mountains. Let him which is on the housetop not come down to take anything out of his house. Neither let him that is in the field return back to take his clothes. And woe unto them that are with child, and to them that give suck in those days. But

pray ye that your flight be not in winter, neither on the Sabbath day. For then shall be great Tribulation such as was not since the beginning of the world to this time, no, nor ever shall be. And except those days should be shortened, there should be no flesh saved. But for the elect's sake those days shall be shortened.

Matthew 24:14-22

On earth those 144,000 completed Jews will experience the plagues Jesus described as a "great distress unequaled from the beginning of the world until now, and never to be equaled again." Jesus told these Christian Jews to leave Palestine, to flee without looking back. They do flee. They scatter across the face of the globe. Those Christians will be God's witnesses to His acts of judgment during the next three and a half years.

If those 144,000 Jews are the only Christians on earth, what has happened to the other hundreds of thousands of believers?

Revelation 7:9-17
The Martyred Christian Welcomed home

Revelation 14:6-16
The Harvest of Martyred Souls

In Revelation 14:6 John referred to an "angel" who represented the evangelists who had the "everlasting Gospel to preach to those that dwell on earth, to every nation, kindred, tongue and people." We know who those evangelists will be. They will be the immortal saints sent back from heaven to preach the Word. John saw them in chapter six when they were sent out from heaven. In chapter fourteen he sees them return- ing to heaven. Their mission has been completed. The last soul has been won. The last Christian has been martyred.

It is of these martyrs that John wrote in the two passages before us. In 14:4 it is Jesus Christ himself, the Son of Man, the one who holds the sickle in his hand who "reaps the earth." The cry of those martyrs in chapter six, "How long, O Lord, until we too are avenged? is now answered. Their number is complete, and it is a multitudinous number. When John saw them entering into heaven in chapter seven he declared that they were so numerous that no man could number them. (7:9) They must have numbered in the millions. We will see too that these are not difficult to identify if we simply accept what John said about them.

Two things are evident. None of them were believers at the time of the Rapture or they would have been caught up to heaven. All of them were saved sometime during those three and a half years from the Rapture to midpoint in the Tribulation. Chapter seven is that midpoint.

The formidable task of evangelizing the entire world will be completed by the evangelists represented by the rider on the white horse in Revelation 6:2.   I sincerely expect to be one of those missionary/evangelists sent back from heaven to complete this worldwide evangelistic effort. I will be terribly disappointed if I get to heaven and discover that I am not coming back to complete the work I was not able to finish during my mortal years on earth.

If you are left behind at the Rapture, I prayerfully hope that you will be one of the millions John told about in chapter seven of Revelation. The Gospel will be preached. You will have an opportunity to hear it. Jesus said, "The Gospel would be preached in all the world for a witness unto all nations, and then shall the end come."

The end is about to come. The period of judgment mixed with grace has come to a close. The final three and a half years of the relentless wrath of God is about to strike mankind. Before that final judgment begins, those believers saved after the Rapture are resurrected and swept into the presence of God. It is this welcoming home scene that John describes in chapter seven. There is no doubt as to who these are. "These are they who have come out of the Great Tribulation. They have washed their robes and made them white in the blood of the Lamb." There is no question as to where they are. "They are before the throne of God, and serve Him day and night in His temple."

If you want a glimpse of the bright side of the apocalypse, listen to the promise of sweet comfort given to these who have come through such incredible suffering and martyrdom. "Never again will they hunger, never again will they thirst. The sun will never beat upon them nor any scorching heat -- and God will wipe away every tear from their eyes."

That covers all the material in chapter seven; but there are a few matters in chapter fourteen to consider before we go.

Revelation 14:8-2
A Preview of the Impending Armageddon

Verses eight through eleven describe precisely what will happen in the next chapters dealing with the trumpets and bowls, the fall of

Babylon. Verses seventeen through twenty describe the battle of Armageddon and the final events of the Tribulation. These two paragraphs are a preview of what is about to happen as the seventh seal is opened and the second half of the Tribulation begins.

We are about to experience through the eyes of John the unbelievable confrontation between God and Satan as Jesus Christ wrestles from Satan the authority over this world and restores the planet Earth to be a suitable place to be called the "footstool of God" and the habitation of Jesus Christ and His redeemed people.

You and I will return to this planet to live for at least a thousand years immediately following three and a half years of unprecedented violence and destruction. The forces of nature will be turned against mankind and the world's diabolical leaders. The purpose is to redeem the purchased possession. Satan is to be evicted and this earth is to be completely renovated. Our world will be renewed and restored in an act of creative redemption. "Behold I make all things new," said Jesus.

In these coming chapters I will endeavor to clarify the confusion seen in most studies of this book of prophecy. Remember, John is telling the same story twice; once from the viewpoint of heaven and again from here on earth. There are parallel chapters covering the same material, so don't be confused if we study these parallel chapters together.

Chapter eight recounts the seven last plagues -- the blowing of the seven trumpets. However, this story is not complete without the corresponding parallel chapter.

The chapter that corresponds to the seven trumpets is chapter sixteen, which overlaps exactly the plagues of chapters eight through eleven. The chart outlining the Book of Revelation illustrates this very clearly. The trumpets and the bowls are the same. While John is standing in heaven witnessing the scene, he sees seven angels with seven trumpets. In chapter sixteen when he returns to earth to retell the story as he sees it from here, he looks up to heaven and observes the mouth of those trumpets which he describes as seven bowls that are poured out. The plagues are identical as we shall see as we look at them in detail.

THE BRIGHT SIDE OF THE APOCALYPSE
LESSON X

DIVISION THREE

Final preparations in
heaven for the renova-
tion of the earth
The first four Trumpets

Chapter 8:1-13

DIVISION FOUR

Final preparation in
heaven for the renova-
tion of earth
Chapter 15:1-8
The first four Bowls

Chapter 16:1-9

REVELATION

CHAPTERS EIGHT, FIFTEEN AND SIXTEEN

If you were to read a hundred and fifty
commentaries and books written to interpret the

meaning of the plagues of the trumpets and the bowls, you would find some very weird explanations and very little agreement among writers who portend to be Bible authorities. Most of what you read would be confusing and contradictory. You would find very little in their writings about which to be elated. Not many people see the bright side of the apocalypse.

Frankly I have not found any studies of the Book of Revelation that interpret the meaning of these chapters in quite the same manner as I do. I do not claim to be the ultimate authority, but after more than thirty-five years of study and teaching this material I am convinced that I have a viewpoint worth sharing with the Christian community.

The seventh and last seal of the scroll John described in chapter five is about to be broken. That document declares Christ to be the rightful owner of planet Earth. He first created it and then redeemed it by paying the price of the purchased possession. The Book of Revelation is the unveiling of a beautiful plan to redeem and restore this world. It is not a plan of chaos and destruction.

For Satan and his people, these chapters are filled with horror and terror. Satan will be forcibly evicted. The accumulated trash of 6000 years of his reign will be consumed by fire. Every trace of sin's contamination will be eradicated. There will be much pain and misery. Most studies of the Book of Revelation dwell on this suffering inflicted on the inhabitants of the world as if this suffering were the end purpose of it all. The suffering John describes is not God's judgment on mankind. God doesn't want any of us to be here. There is no need for any of us to remain on earth and receive the agonizing blows this planet is about to receive. You needn't be here. Today when you see what is about to happen, respond to God's love, yield to his will, accept his mercy. Call upon him and you will be saved. "Now is the day of salvation." You can be ready at the Rapture and caught up with Christ in the air. Even to those who miss the Rapture, God will extend his hand of mercy and forgiveness. He is not willing that any should perish, but that all should come to repentance. Though millions have come still there is room -- There is room at the cross for you.

Every person living on earth will be confronted by the evangelists during the first half of the Tribulation and given an opportunity to accept God's love and forgiveness. Obviously everyone will not repent. Hundreds of millions will choose a life of immorality, hedonism and worldliness. They will choose to receive the mark of the beast. They will choose to align themselves with Satan and Antichrist. They will choose their own destiny just as I have chosen mine.

That destiny for them is an eternity in hell. The three and a half years of the final seven plagues is not God's judgment against mankind. There will be a judgment. There will be a day of reckoning and there will be an eternal hell for all those who reject Jesus Christ. These three and a half years are not that hell. Granted millions of human beings will be violently killed in these cataclysmic events that are about to happen. Only a very small percentage of the five billion inhabitants of planet Earth will survive. Yet nothing that any of them will suffer can compare with the eternal burning hell that awaits every one of those who chooses to reject Christ. The theme of the Book of Revelation is not destruction. It is redemption. That process of redemption is painful.

Revelation 8:1-6
Final Preparation in Revelation 15:1-8
Heaven for the Renovation of Earth

Chapter eight begins with a period of silence in heaven. It is a worship service. Chapter 15 in its entirety describes this reunion. All of us, the redeemed, will be present. The only Christians absent are the 144,000 born again Jews who were sealed by the Holy Spirit and dispersed across the face of the earth. Very possibly the prayer of the saints mentioned in 8:3 and 4 are prayers offered for those 144,000 brothers and sisters who remained on earth and will experience the horror of total devastation. When John describes this scene in chapter 15 he gives details that are not in chapter eight. He especially mentions that he saw a multitude of those who had been victorious over the beast and his image. Again they sang the song of Moses.

John also mentions that just before the trumpets sounded and the bowls were poured out, the temple in heaven was filled with smoke of the glory of God and no one could enter the temple until the seven plagues of the seven angels was completed. (Revelation 15:5-8) We will see the significance of that statement when the temple is opened again after the seven last plagues in Revelation 11:19.

At the end of the half hour of silent prayers and the singing of the song of Moses, the angel with the golden censer fills it with coals from the altar of God and hurls it onto earth and there resounds peals of thunder, rumblings, flashes of lightning and an earthquake. God is serving notice on Satan that the end is near.

It is the end of Satan and his cohorts of

which we speak, not the end of the world. God has no intention of destroying or allowing this world to be destroyed. The apocalypse does not signify the end of the world, but the end of evil. During that period of three and a half years there will be tremendous ecological upheavals that will change the face of the earth and the earth's climate. Never forget that immediately after the Tribulation Christ and His saints will return to this very planet and begin the millennial reign of our Lord on earth. For that reason I cannot accept that these final plagues of the seven trumpets and seven bowls represent nuclear war. If such were the case, the world that would be left at the end of three and a half years of thermonuclear warfare would be a radioactive cinder and not the paradise that Christ promised His people. I cannot imagine a nuclear war that would last for three and a half years. It could be three and a half hours maybe; or even three and a half days; but not three and a half years. These seven last plagues are not thermonuclear warfare; but something else, totally different. What happens next is not nation against nation. It is God Almighty's intervention. We read about it in chapters eight through eleven and sixteen. Let's look at it through the writings of John.

THE FIRST TRUMPET/BOWL

**Revelation 8:7 The first angel sounded and

there followed hail and fire mingled with blood and they were cast upon the earth, and the third part of the trees was burned up and all green grass was burned up.

Revelation 16:2   And the first went and poured out his vial upon the earth and there fell a noisome and grevious sore upon the men which had the mark of the beast and upon those who worshipped his image.

In chapter eight John is in heaven looking down upon the earth below. He can see the terrible conflagration as one third of the earth and all the green grass is burned up. John described a fire of unbelievable proportions as burning coals rain down from heaven and cover the entire planet. Probably John is describing a shower of meteorites that will penetrate our earth's atmosphere. As the world rotates in the path of this bombardment from outer space, every continent in its path will burn with a rain of fire. That fire is for a purpose. The planet is to be purged from the blight of sin.

We cannot imagine how deeply the curse of sin has contaminated our earth. All thorns, weeds, thistles, harmful insects, bacteria and viruses will be purged from the earth's soil. That could be the purpose of this worldwide burn. Maybe this is the fire described in II Peter 3:10.

A secondary result of this first plague affects the people. It went unnoticed by John as he looked down from heaven, but in chapter 16 he is on earth. What John saw were terrible sores on many, if not all those people, who received the mark of the beast. Those sores could very well be radiation burns from the nuclear war that had recently taken place.

THE SECOND TRUMPET/BOWL

Revelation 8:8 And the second angel sounded and as it were a great mountain burning with fire was cast into the sea and a third part of the sea became blood.

Revelation 16:3 And   the second angel poured out his vial upon the sea and it became as blood of a dead man, and every living soul died in the sea.

At the sounding of the second and third trumpets, two great meteors the size of mountains strike the earth. The first lands in the sea; the other strikes a land area. To understand the purpose of these two meteors we must reconstruct how the earth was at creation. Scientists have studied that question for years and have given us much insight.

They tell us that the world in which we live today is not as it was when God created it. We don't know when or how that change came about, but it was a violent change. Our planet today is inclined 23 degrees on its axis. It is that inclination that gives us the frozen polar regions. It was not always so. Frozen prehistoric animals have been discovered in the polar regions with tropical vegetation still in their stomachs. It appears that their habitat was suddenly covered over by tremendous tidal waves and   that water froze immediately to a phenomenal depth, entrapping these animals just as they existed those many years ago. How many years ago, no one has been able to pinpoint.

The Antarctic region at the south pole is a continent. It is an ice enshrouded land mass. It was at one time a tropical area covered over by dense jungle vegetation. We know that to be true without question. The reason we know is that today the Chilean government is pumping crude oil from wells on that frozen Antarctic continent not many miles from the south pole. One of the world's largest beds of coal lies beneath the ice of Antarctica. That oil and coal are there from decayed jungle vegetation that must have flourished millions of years ago on that southern continent of Antarctica. The change came about by a sudden shift of the earth's axis, probably several millions of years ago.

The massive deserts of Africa, Asia and South America are a direct result of this inclination of the earth's axis. I have crossed the desert of northern Chile many times. That desert is a layer of salt four to six feet deep. It obviously was once an ocean floor. I walked one day along what appeared to be a sandy beach that extended for many miles along the Pacific ocean. Hundreds of thousands of sea shells covered that particular beach. The unbelievable truth is, that that desert sea bed and that beautiful, isolated shell covered beach are today more than 3000 feet above sea level.

What happened to this planet Earth to change a tropical jungle into a frozen ice pack and lift a beautiful beach 3000 feet out of the water? We have evidence of what happened in Crater Lake Arizona; and in similar craters in Siberia and other parts of the world. Meteorites of sufficient size struck the earth with enough impact to tilt the planet on its axis and to drive it several thousand miles further from the sun from where it was at creation.

Can you imagine living on this planet when such a fantastic upheaval is taking place? It is doubtful that any human beings were living on this planet when those first meteorites struck the earth's surface. Obviously there would have been incredible tidal waves and earthquakes as continents were shifted and mountains were pushed up from the surface of the earth.

In the story of creation we discover in Genesis 1:9 a fascinating observation -- "And God said, let the water under the sky be gathered together to **one place,** and let dry ground appear." There was a time when there was only one land mass and probably many times more land surface than what there is today. This observation coincides with the scientific theory that North and South America were once joined to Europe and Africa but have separated, and even today continue to drift apart.

There was another difference before the flood. Genesis 1:6 says "Let there be an expanse between the waters to separate water from water... and God called the expanse sky." What the Bible is describing here is a phenomenon that no longer exists. The world before the flood was enveloped in a dense water vapor that covered the entire globe, protecting the earth from the sun's harmful radiation and producing a "green house" effect over the entire planet. Since the earth then was in an orbit much closer to the sun, that canopy of water vapor served to protect the surface of the earth from dangerous solar radiation. It also served to diffuse the heat of the sun over the polar regions resulting in a tropical climate over the entire face of the planet. Vegetation flourished profusely.

Early in the Book of Genesis there was no rain. Mist and dew watered the earth. When the first rains fell at the time of the great flood, the expanse of water that enveloped the world was poured out on the earth. "The floodgates of the heavens were opened." It rained forty days and forty nights. That water never returned to replenish the expanse of water in the sky. It will be replaced, however, when God restores this planet to the kind of world He created as a paradise for humankind. That change will take place during the three and a half years described in chapters eight through eleven and sixteen.

When the second angel sounds the trumpet and pours out the second bowl, a tremendous meteorite will strike the planet. John described it as a huge mountain that landed in the sea. The force of the impact of that meteor will correct the angle of the earth's axis from the present 23 degrees to perpendicular. Can you imagine what this will do to the oceans of the world? Can you envision the resulting tidal waves? The Bible speaks a special warning to those who live on the coasts. "Woe to those who live by the sea." Jesus speaking of that day in Luke 21:25 told of the sea and the waves roaring. Cities like Los Angeles, Tokyo, Buenos Aires, Le Harve, Hongkong, Singapore will be totally annihilated by 100 foot tsunamis. Incredible as it may seem, the human race will survive although millions will lose their lives in these catastrophes.

It is interesting in Revelation 8:8 that John observes "one third of the living creatures in the sea died and a third of the ships were destroyed. Then in 15:3 when he is describing the same event he declares, "Every living thing in the sea died." At first reading this may sound like a contradiction of fact. The difference, however, is in the point of view. In chapter 8 John is in heaven looking down on the entire planet Earth. He can see from that vantage point that one third of the living creatures in the sea died. In chapter sixteen John is standing on earth near the point of impact and he observed that from what he saw there, every living creature in the sea died. These subtle differences in the two accounts serve to convince me that my theory is correct -- the plagues of the trumpets and the bowls are the same.

Let us read on as the third angel sounds his trumpet and pours out his bowl.

THE THIRD TRUMPET/BOWL

Revelation 8:10,11   And the third angel sounded and there fell a great star from heaven, burning as it were a lamp. And it fell upon the third part of the rivers and upon the fountains of water.

Revelation16:4 And the third angel poured out his vial upon the rivers and fountains and they became blood.

If you look carefully at the wording of these two passages, you can pinpoint where this meteor will strike. Evidently this great star, blazing like a torch, strikes the earth at some point where it contaminated the headwaters of a great river system. One third of the earth's total rivers flowed from that fountain. There is only one river that qualifies -- the Amazon.

I was in Peru the year of the worldwide geodetic survey sponsored by the United Nations. I talked with a group of engineers who were endeavoring to determine the volume and flow of the Amazon river. When they sounded the Amazon at Iquitos in Peru, 3,000 miles upstream from the mouth of the river, they discovered to their amazement that at that point the Amazon was more than 650 feet deep. These engineers concluded from all their studies that the volume of flow in the Amazon river is 200 times greater than was ever calculated before the survey.

This immense river system originates at the confluence of three Peruvian rivers -- the Ucayali, the Huallaga and the Maranon. These three rivers have a common source, a lake high in the Andes Mountains in southern Peru. Of course there are other great rivers like the Rio Negro that flow into the Amazon after it is formed, but the three rivers I have named are the headwaters of the Amazon river system.

It could very well be that the point of impact of this second meteor will be somewhere in the Andes mountains. The place is only speculation. The fact that it will happen is not speculation. The meteor that will strike the earth somewhere near the equator will drive our world thousands of miles closer to the sun to the position in solar orbit where it was placed at the time of original creation. What a day that will be. Can you better see now what is the purpose of these so called plagues of the trumpets and bowls? Maybe "plagues" is a poor translation of the Greek word "plege" which means to strike or to pound. God is pounding this world into shape. He is not yet finished. The fourth angel is about to sound his trumpet and pour out his bowl.

THE FOURTH TRUMPET/BOWL

Revelation 8:12 And the fourth angel sounded and the third part of the sun was smitten, and the third part of the moon and the third part of the stars, so the third part of them was darkened and the day shone not for the third part of it and the night likewise.

Revelation 16:8, 9 And the fourth angel poured out his vial upon the sun; and power was given unto him to scorch men with fire. And men were scorched with great heat and blasphemed the name of God which had power over these plagues. And they repented not to give him glory.

Here is another phenomenon of nature that could be a drama out of the "Twilight Zone." The temperature of the earth's surface vacillates between extreme hot and extreme cold. Dense clouds of dust and smoke will blacken the sky. That huge cloud mass will be from the smoke and ash of the worldwide burn and erupting volcanoes caused by the earth's shifting surfaces. We have experienced such clouds of ash and smoke from the burning Kuwait oil fields, Mount St. Helens and Pinatubo, but these are insignificant in comparison to what John described. That dense cloud will enshroud a third of the earth's surface. As the cloud orbits the earth it will totally obscure the light of the sun and stars. In those cloud covered areas the world will be in pitch darkness and in sub-zero temperatures.

At the same time that part of the world not covered by that cloud will experience intense searing heat caused by the planet's new position in solar orbit much closer to the sun. In chapter eight John is in heaven observing that massive dense cloud. In chapter sixteen he is on earth describing the intense searing heat. This scorching heat serves a very definite purpose in God's operation to restore the climate of the world to what it was at creation. Hundreds of millions of gallons of sea water will be evaporated and sucked up into the atmosphere to restore the water expanse in the heavens above the earth, just as it was described in Genesis 1:6-8.This is what John calls "the new heaven." He is not talking about the abode of God, but rather about the renewal of the "first heaven" the sky above the earth, the firmament, the earth's atmosphere. Our world's atmosphere has been contaminated, polluted, and nearly depleted. What happens through the action of this fourth angel is absolutely essential for the restoration of our world.

This creative act of restoration and renewal is the bright side of the apocalypse that I don't find even mentioned in most studies of the Book of Revelation. When we see the purposes of these acts of God we can better see what happened in chapters eight and sixteen. When God is finished with His job of renovation our world will be restored to a tropical paradise shielded by a special atmosphere to protect the earth's surface from the intense heat of the sun and all harmful radiation from outer space.

No one was present to witness the original creation of the world. There will, however, be people living on earth to witness this recreation as Jesus Christ "makes all things new."John was there and he saw it In chapter sixteen he observed the reaction of the people around him. They knew it was God working, but "they blasphemed His name and repented not to give Him glory." Certainly these so called plagues that resulted from the sounding of the first four trumpets and the outpouring of the first four bowls will have devastating effect on the lives of the people living on earth. Many will die. Many will suffer grave injuries. There will be tremendous loss in terms of human suffering. It is important to remember that these four plagues are not directed toward Antichrist, the false prophet or their followers. God's first concern is the restoration of the earth to its created state. It is part of the process of making all things new. These will be tremendous miracles that God performs to purge the earth of every vestige of sin. The earth will be the kingdom of Jesus Christ. Not one acre of ground or one city lot belongs to any human being. We think it does. We act like it does. The inhabitants of this world will not readily surrender their claim to possession. I am sure God's heart is grieved at the callouse stubborn attitude of mankind. For two thousand years he has sent prophets, priests, missionaries, pastors, evangelists and thousands of dedicated laymen to appeal to a lost world of sinners. It isn't that God does not love the sinner. But what more can He do to save them. They have rejected His Son and His message of love and salvation. The day of judgment has come. God is preparing the world for the kingdom age -- the millennium. When the angel sounds the fourth trumpet and pours out the fourth bowl, that work will be about completed.

The last three plagues are very different from the first four. They are not directed against the planet. Actually we will see that these plagues are not from God at all. It will be Satan himself who turns against the inhabitants of his own kingdom. God merely steps aside and allows him to do it. Before the fifth angel sounds his trumpet John heard an angel flying through the midst of heaven saying with a loud voice, "Woe, woe, woe to the inhabitants of the earth".

THE BRIGHT SIDE OF THE APOCALYPSE

LESSON XI

DIVISION FOUR

The rise of Antichrist
The rise of the False
Prophet

Chapter 13

DIVISION FIVE

The Mystery of Babylon
The ten nations set out to
destroy the false church

Chapters 17 and 18

REVELATION CHAPTER SEVENTEEN
(Parallel chapter thirteen)

We studied the Raptured Church and the
Tribulation Church in Divisions Three and Four.

Now we will study the satanic church lead by the false prophet. Of course the millions of people from every nation on earth who will belong to this organization will not call it a satanic church. To them Antichrist will be the true Messiah. I call the head of that church the false prophet, but that will not be his title, nor how his followers perceive him. Even though he will be powerful and ruthless, the masses will follow him devotedly. He will have a winsome personality, mystical supernatural powers, and will be dramatically persuasive.

The church will be the social arm of the secular government, providing for the basic needs of the poor, the minorities, the handicapped, and all such who need someone to champion their cause. That church will be extremely wealthy and generous. The false prophet will have no difficulty winning allegiance to his cause.

We were first introduced to the leader of that church in chapter thirteen. We call him the false prophet. He is in reality a powerful fallen angel who ascends out of the bottomless pit in the center of the earth and takes on the form of a human being. He is not a man, he never was a man. He never will be a man. He is a fallen angel, a demon spirit. Chapters seventeen and eighteen give us more insight into this demonic leader and the satanic church which he directs.

 Revelation 17:1-6
The Mystery of Babylon the Great
The Mother of Harlots
And the False Prophet

In the first verse of chapter seventeen one of the angels who had the seven last plagues took John to a place where he could observe what the angel called, "the whore that sitteth upon many waters."

There are two symbols in that statement. Fortunately the angel interpreted both of them. Verse 15 says

The waters which thou sawest, where the whore sitteth, are peoples, and multitudes, and nations and tongues.

What a degrading term used by the angel to describe a church -- "the great whore." In the Bible the terms whore, harlot and adulteress are frequently used to symbolize the people who have forsaken the true and living God to follow after false gods and idols.

The symbol of the woman is further explained in verse 18.

And the woman which thou sawest is that great city, which reigneth over the kings of the earth.

That is not a woman in the sense of the female species of the human race. She is a city. But which city. There is only one city named in this chapter, Babylon. That woman had the name Babylon written on her forehead. The entire eighteenth chapter deals exculsively with the destruction of the city of Babylon.

In the Book of Revelation Babylon is the city most often identified with the false church, that ancient city located on the plains of Shinar on the Euphrates river in the country we know today as Iraq. Babylon was previously called Babel. It was there the massive brick tower was built to reach heaven. The ancient Babylonians did not presume that they could enter heaven by scaling their monstrous tower. They built that tower to provide a platform from which they could study the heavens. It was the Babylonians who introduced the concept of astrology -- the pagan belief that the destinies of man are determined by the configuration of the stars.

Babylon became the third world empire after Egypt and Assyria. The Jews were taken there in captivity in the days of Ezra, Daniel,

Nehemiah, and Queen Esther. It is no mystery where Babylon is located. The mystery is whether this is the city to which John referred in his Revelation. Many Bible scholars sincerely believe that the ancient city of Babylon will be rebuilt and restored to a world center of commerce. There are others of us who disagree.

In chapter seventeen John referred to the "seat of Satan," which in Bible times was ancient Babylon. Every cult and every false religion in the world can trace its source to Babylon. At one time Babylon was the seat of Satan.   However, in Revelation 2:13 Christ said of the Church of Pergamos, "I know where thou dwellest, even where Satan's seat is." Pergamos represented the period 312 A.D. to 540 A.D.   when Emperor Constantine converted to Christianity and Rome became the headquarters city of the church. It was Rome, not Babylon, that was the "seat of Satan."

Satan must have a city where he is located. He is not God. He is not omnipresent. He is one person and can only be at one place at a time. The headquarters of Satan has not always remained in one place. I do not know where it is located now, but I do know that during the Tribulation the seat of Satan will not be the Iraqi city of Babylon on the Euphrates river. I believe the false prophet will direct the false church from the city of Rome. Verse nine further identifies the city where the woman sitteth as the city of seven mountains. Rome is known everywhere as the city that sits on seven hills.

Cities do not rule the world. Washington and Moscow do not rule over anybody. It is the people who are represented by those cities who wield the power. That is the meaning of 17:18. The angel referred to the leaders headquartered there, and not to the buildings. Those leaders are Antichrist and the false prophet. We met both of them in our study of chapter thirteen and we meet them again here in chapter seventeen.

In verse 3 John saw the woman, which is the false church, carried on the back of the scarlet colored beast with seven heads and ten horns. From what we saw in chapter thirteen, this is Antichrist. He is pictured carrying the false church. The false prophet is supported by and dependent upon the secular leader, Antichrist. Verse 4 described the riches and wealth that this relationship generated for the abominable church. It was evidently a comfortable and profitable relationship. In return for those material benefits the false prophet and his people served Antichrist by spearheading the relentless attack of persecution of the followers of Christ, the true church. In verse 6 John described the false church as being drunken with the blood of the martyrs of Jesus.

Revelation 17:7-15
The Harlot of Babylon
The False Prophet

In this section John explained the relationship that existed between Antichrist and the false prophet. No correct interpretation can be made of this chapter unless you clearly distinguish between those two personalities.

We saw in chapter thirteen that Antichrist is the first beast that came out of the sea of humanity. (13:1) He has seven heads and ten horns and upon his horns ten crowns. (13:1 and 17:7) The seven heads represent seven world empires: Egypt, Assyria, Babylon, Persia, Greece, Rome and the second Roman empire of the Tribulation. Antichrist is the ruler of the seventh. The ten horns are the ten rulers of the principle countries that will make up the reconstructed Roman empire. Periodically we can see these heads of state on television today.

The second beast rises out of the earth. He ascends out of the abyss called the bottomless pit. (13:11, 11:7 and 17:8) He is described in 17:8 as "the beast that was, and is not, and shall ascend out of the bottomless pit." Here is the meaning of that curious verse. This being was once a holy angel. He had been a devoted servant of God. When Satan rebelled against God and was cast out of heaven this fallen angel was incarcerated in the bottomless pit somewhere in the center of the earth. During the Tribulation he is to be set loose for a short time and will take the form of a human being. The false prophet will build his own empire worldwide which John called in 17:8 the eighth kingdom which will be part of the seventh.

Verse 12 tells how the ten nations of Europe will give their support to the false prophet in his effort to destroy the true church. "These will make war on the Lamb," John said. Hundreds of thousands of Christians will be killed. It will look like the forces of evil prevail, but that is not so. Verse 14 says, "The Lamb will overcome them." Instead of diminishing from the murderous activities of the death squads the Christians multiplied to become millions. The saints who will come back to earth from heaven will thwart the evil designs of the false prophet and his allies with strikes, sabotage and work stoppages. The economy of the European Community will plummet in free fall. Business leaders and government administrators will not know what hit them. Yes, the Lamb will overcome.

At midpoint in the seven year Tribulation a dramatic change will occur. We saw it in our study of chapters seven and fourteen. The millions of born again believers who were converted after the Rapture will be swept into heaven. The evangelists will be called back to heaven and there will no longer be a true church for the false prophet to persecute. The only believers on earth during the second half of the Tribulation will be the 144,000 converted Jews and their number will be insignificant since they will be scattered across the face of the entire planet.

When the true church has been taken out of the world, the satanic church will no longer serve any purpose and a dramatic turnaround will take place. There will develop a rift between the false prophet and the leaders of the ten nations. It is a development that is often overlooked in our study of the end times. We overlook it because we fail to consider the three parallel sections together.

Revelation 17:16-18
The Ten Nations of Europe
Set out to Destroy the False Church

Read verse 16 carefully. All ten nations of the European Economic Community will turn on the church of Rome because that organization has become a parasite in their eyes. "Those ten nations will hate the whore and shall eat her flesh and burn her with fire."

That verse describes exactly what will happen when the fifth angel sounds his trumpet and pours out his bowl. We can see the unfolding of that dramatic story when we put all the pieces of the account together from the parallel Scriptures found in nine, sixteen and eighteen. These three chapters relate the closing events of the Tribulation -- the final three plagues of the trumpets and bowls.

THE BRIGHT SIDE OF THE APOCALYPSE

LESSON XII

DIVISION THREE

The Fifth Trumpet
The Sixth Trumpet

Chapter 9:1-21

DIVISION FOUR

The Fifth Bowl
The Sixth Bowl

Chapter 16:10-16

DIVISION FIVE

The Beast of Babylon
Satan's attack on Rome
The Fall of Rome

Chapter 18:1-24

REVELATION CHAPTER EIGHTEEN
(Parallel Chapters Nine and Sixteen)

Revelation 9:1-12
The Demons from the Abyss

Revelation 16:10, 11

The Attack on the Beast

Revelation 18:1-14
The Fall of Babylon

The final events of the Tribulation begin in Revelation 9:1 when the fifth angel sounds his trumpet and John says, "I saw a star fall from heaven unto earth." A better translation is "I saw a star that had fallen from the sky to earth." This "star" of 9:1 obviously is not a literal star or heavenly body, but rather a star in the sense of a celebrity. I believe this star is the same one described by the prophet in Isaiah 14:12 as Lucifer or the "star of the morning." It is Satan himself -- the one cast out of heaven long before the first man ever appeared on earth.

Jesus Christ gives to Satan the key to the bottomless pit. We know according to Revelation 1:18 that Jesus possesses that key. John then tells us that Satan opened the pit and unleashed its demonic inhabitants. Those demon spirits could be the fallen angels we are told about in II Peter 2:4.

For if God spared not the angels that sinned, but cast them down to hell and delivered them in chains of darkness to be reserved unto judgment.   II Peter2:4

These particular fallen angels are so ferocious that God has kept them bound since the days of Noah. Their leader is evidently a powerful angel with authority and power nearly as great as that of Satan. His name is Abbadon and Apollyon meaning destroyer. At the present time he is in a place called the abyss or the bottomless pit, located somewhere in the bowels of the earth.

There are two things I would like you to see concerning Satan, Apollyon and their followers:

(1) Satan and Apollyon are powerful. Yet with all their power they are still subject to the authority of God. When Jesus Christ says to Satan, "Come up here and get the key" he goes up and gets it. In no way has Satan taken control. He and all his fallen angels are subject to the will of God and always will be. It is Jesus Christ himself who orders Satan to open the abyss and to direct the attack of those demons against the seat of the beast.

(2) The second observation is that Satan is the eternal enemy of man. He is against God and all His creation. You cannot rely on Satan to be your friend simply because you are his follower.In Revelation chapter nine, every inhabitant on earth, except the 144,000 sealed ones, are

followers of Antichrist. They have taken the mark of the beast and have pledged to him their allegiance. They are his people. Yet, it is Satan who turns against the false prophet and the millions who follow him. There seems to be no honor among thieves. Don't be too quick to blame God when you see the misery of war plaguing the human race.

Once we identify these characters in chapter nine, sixteen and eighteen, it will not be difficult to understand the scenario John describes.

When the bottomless pit was opened dense smoke billowed from the hole. Out of that smoke came a horde of locust with the sting of scorpions. These are not ordinary locust. Their mission is not to devour the green grass of the fields, nor the leaves of the trees and bushes. They are not locusts at all. They are demon spirits, and like all demonic spirits they have the capacity to take up residence in human beings. It is called demon possession. That army that will march across Europe will not be a cloud of buzzing locusts but an army of demon possessed men. The description that John gives us in Revelation 9:7-10 could very well be that of helicopters and other machinery of modern day warfare, for John is describing a modern army of the European nations.

We know from verse ten of chapter nine that the campaign of this army will last five months. However, we do not know from the reading of chapter nine whom they are going to attack. It is only as we read the parallel Scripture in chapter sixteen that we will discover the answer to this dilemma.

Revelation 16:10, 11
The Fifth Bowl

Here John vividly describes the excruciating pain of the sting of those locust/scorpion. He gives us further insight as to who will be attacked. "...The seat of the beast and his kingdom."

However, there are two beasts. Both the Antichrist and the false prophet are beasts. (Revelation 13:1 and 11) The Antichrist is the beast that emerges from the sea of humanity and the false prophet is the beast out of the earth from the bottomless pit. To which of these is John referring in 16:10? To get the answer we must look at the final piece of the puzzle in the third parallel passage -- Revelation chapter eighteen.

Revelation 18:1-4
The Beast of Babylon

This chapter opens with the appearance of a brilliant angel whose splendor illuminates the earth. He shouts in a voice that can be heard by all and pronounces a grave indictment against Babylon the seat of the false church. We discussed already the hatred and jealousy that had evolved among the ten nations of Europe against the false prophet. We know from reading 17:12 and 17:16 that all the ten nations of Europe hate the false church and set themselves to attack her center in Rome and "make her desolate, naked, to eat her flesh and burn her with fire." We are now seeing the consummation of that anger. Apollyon leads this army of destruction against the false prophet and his false church. His objective is to destroy the church headquarters in Rome. That is what takes place in chapter eighteen.

Verses two and three are a graphic description of that church as God saw it "...habitation of devils" "...hold of every foul spirit" "...cage of every unclean and hateful bird." He goes on to describe the church's pernicious dealings with the kings of the world through which it gained unlimited wealth. The church of the false prophet will have no worries about raising money for its support.This church will have at its disposition the wealth of the mighty, worldwide police state of Antichrist.

In verse four the angel issues a warning to the Lord's people who might be living in Rome. These could only be some of the 144,000 for they are the only people God has living on earth when these events takes place.

The eternal city of Rome is about to be destroyed. That destruction will come from an army possessed by demon spirits released from the abyss and led by Apollyon the destroyer.

Revelation 18:5-20
Satan's Attack on Rome

Although the march across Europe to Rome will take five months, (9:5) the climactic destruction will take only one hour and will leave the city a burning ruin. (18:9,10) Some of those structures that will be reduced to rubble have endured since the first century. Verses eleven through twenty are a lament pronounced by the world for the terrible destruction of this magnificent world capital. In that lament there is a spectacular inventory of wealth and of commodities bought and sold through Rome. John makes a horrible addition at the end of that list in verse thirteen. "...And slaves and the souls of men."

The meaning of this verse is that men and

women will literally sell their souls to Satan in return for his favors. That is what receiving the mark of the beast will amount to. To receive that mark is to sell your soul and seal your doom. Once you bear that mark there is no possibility of ever being redeemed. Even though it will cost you your life, refuse to take that mark.

Revelation 18:21-24
The Fall of Rome

In a demonstration given by another angel in 18:21 we are given some idea how Rome was destroyed. This angel picked up a boulder the size of a millstone and threw it into the sea. "...With such violence will this great city be thrown down, never to be found again." In John's day, of course, there were no weapons capable of destroying a city in one blow. Armies besieged a city over a period of weeks and months. Finally they would sack and burn it. They had no means to destroy an entire city the size of Rome in an hour's time. For us in the twentieth century however, it is not difficult to interpret the angel's demonstration of a boulder cast into the sea.

The final verses of chapter eighteen are a funeral dirge sung by a mighty angel as he pronounces the eternal doom of this so-called "eternal city of Rome."

These particular passages of the Book of Revelation that we have just studied are the most difficult in the entire book to interpret. You will find very few Bible studies that will give you a clear understanding of this section in the Revelation.

How beautiful it is when you are able to fit the pieces of the puzzle together and finally see a clear picture emerging. I recognized several years ago that there are these parallel sections in the Book of Revelation, each covering the same period from the Rapture to the Second Coming. At first I was not aware of how important and how reliable was that particular key to interpretation. The hordes of demon locusts under Apollyon in chapters nine and sixteen are not such a mystery in the light of chapter eighteen.

The first woe is past. There are two woes to come. (9:12)

Revelation 9:13-21
The Sixth Trumpet/Bowl

Revelation 16:12-16
Preparation for the Battle of Armageddon

When the sixth trumpet sounds and the sixth bowl is poured out an army of 200 million soldiers begin a march on Palestine from the Orient. They probably come from China. The river Euphrates dries up and provides a roadbed for that vast army marching toward Armageddon.

Who are these 200 million soldiers going to fight? In the sixteenth chapter John tells us of three evil spirits like frogs that come out of the mouth of the dragon. Of course they are not frogs. They are emissaries of Antichrist. They are spokesmen for the dragon, Satan. They will travel from nation to nation, hopping from one capital to another. Their assignment is to secure a pledge of military support from every ally of the European Community. That will be the United States and Canada, the countries of South America, India, Australia, Japan and many more. These are those who will confront that vast Chinese army of 200 million men marching across China, Pakistan, India, Iran and Iraq toward Palestine. All of this is in preparation for the battle of Armageddon. That will be the final great battle that truly can be called the "mother of all battles."

In no way is that battle of Armageddon a nuclear war. The Scripture gives us some interesting insights into that final battle. Evidently we are not reading here of a thermonuclear war. The army of aggression launching an attack in a nuclear war would never march 200 million men onto a battle field.They would dispatch their army to missile silos and ICBM launching pads. They would be at sea on nuclear armed warships and submarines. No, this is not describing nuclear war. Remember, immediately following this battle Jesus Christ is returning to earth and His multiplied millions of followers will occupy this planet. We are not coming back to a planet ravished by nuclear war and totally uninhabitable because of massive radiation. If such were the case, there would be no bright side of the apocalypse. This would be a literal doomsday.

This chapter describes the weapons of warfare and they all appear to be weapons of conventional armament. In Revelation John tells us that one third of the inhabitants of earth will be killed in that battle and we are told how they are killed. (1) by fire, which is some kind of flamethrower, (2) by smoke, which is probably poisonous gas or nerve gas, (3) by brimstone, which is some kind of napalm or anti-personnel bomb.

John also indicates how long this battle will last -- "one hour and a day and a month and a year." (Revelation 9:15) That totals up to 396 days plus one hour. In those thirteen months one third of all the men living on earth will be slain. The world's population has been drastically reduced, but this casualty figure could reach as much as 300 million killed in action. In another verse John tells us that it will take six months to bury the dead from that battle in the valley of Megiddo.

Before the seventh angel sounds his trumpet and pours out his bowl, John inserts two parenthetical chapters dealing with two significant independent events. They are kind of a vignette, a story within a story. Chapter ten gives us further insight into the meaning of the sealed scroll that we studied in chapters five and six. Chapter eleven relates the incredible story of two witnesses who will be killed by the false prophet and subsequently will rise from the dead and ascend into heaven.

Let us look first at chapter ten.

THE BRIGHT SIDE OF THE APOCALYPSE

LESSON XIII

DIVISION THREE

**John is instructed to
eat the scroll**

Chapter 10

REVELATION CHAPTER TEN

**Revelation 10:1-7
The Mighty Angel
Declares that the End is at Hand**

Chapters ten and eleven, the final two chapters of Division Three, are inserted at the close of John's account of the seven year Tribulation. Chapter ten gives us further insight into the meaning of the scroll. That scroll had served its purpose. The earth had been reclaimed from Satan and restored as God's paradise. The entire chapter is a dialogue between the apostle

John and one described as a "mighty angel."

The one described as a Mighty Angel can be none other than Jesus Christ. He is the same one who took the scroll in chapter five. That scroll, the title deed of this planet Earth, is the center of this strange story.

The mighty angel shouts and the echo reverberates back to John as the sound of seven thunders. John is about to record the startling message but a voice from heaven orders him not to write it down.I believe I know what the message was about and why John was told not to record it.

This drama between John and Jesus is a prelude to the coming of Christ. At this point in the book of Revelation the seven years of the Tribulation were about to end. The physical aspect of our planet had been totally changed to a tropical paradise. Already the vast deserts of the world had begun to blossom like a rose as had been prophesied. The ten nations of Europe had turned on the false prophet and had destroyed the satanic church. An army of 200 million men marched on Palestine from China. For more than a year two massive armies had been locked in a bloody conflict on the plains of Megiddo. The skies were about to split and the conquering Christ was poised for his triumphal return. His coming was imminent. His plans were secret. They were not to be revealed. To this day, a thousand years later, Satan does not know what to expect at the coming of Christ. One day you and I will hear the message that resounded across the heavens as the sound of seven thunders, and we will clearly understand what it says. It will be declared for the entire universe to hear.

When the seventh trumpet sounds in chapter eleven the mystery of God will be accomplished. The prophecies of all ages will have been fulfilled. Bible scholars who see the seven trumpets and the seven bowls as separate plagues are here confronted with the statement of 10:7 that at the sounding of the seventh trumpet it will be all over...Christ returns with His saints. If the trumpets and bowls are not the same plagues, you still have to explain the plagues of the seven bowls. This chapter makes it more evident that we are right in seeing the seven trumpets and the seven bowls as describing the same events. John gives this theory of parallel chapters much support.

Revelation 10:8-14
John is instructed to eat the scroll

A voice from heaven told John to take the scroll from the hand of the mighty angel. This scroll is the title deed to our planet. What is happening is tremendous. Satan is about to be forcibly evicted. "There will be no more delay" said the mighty angel in 10:6. "All is in readiness." Chapters nine, eleven, sixteen and nineteen bring us to this climactic moment -- the Second Coming of Christ.

The angel then said to John, "Take the scroll and eat it up."This is symbolic language. More than one prophet of the Old Testament was told to "eat" a scroll of Hebrew Scriptures.The eating is equivalent to hearing and believing the message. In this case when John "ate the scroll" it was sweet in his mouth, but dreadfully sour in his stomach. The message to John is that the Second Coming of Christ is glorious, beautiful and wonderful. He rejoiced at the spectacle of the glorified Christ. But he shuddered when he saw the final and dreadful judgment of God.

The prophet had said many years before, "It is a fearful thing to fall into the hands of an angry God".

THE BRIGHT SIDE OF THE APOCALYPSE

LESSON XIV

DIVISION THREE

The two witnesses

Chapter 11

REVELATION CHAPTER ELEVEN

The story in chapter eleven takes place during the last three and a half years of the Tribulation as indicated in 11:2. These are the 42 months when the holy city will be tread under the feet of the Gentiles. These are the three and a half years of the abomination of desolation beginning midpoint in the seven years of Tribulation. That period begins when the 144,000 were sealed and told to flee from Palestine. Two lonely witnesses were ordered to stay. According to Revelation 11:3 the two prophets were to witness 1260 days which corresponds to the 42 months of verse two.

We know by Revelation 11:1 that John

found these two witnesses in Jerusalem where he was sent to measure the temple. There was no temple when John wrote the Book of Revelation. It had been destroyed in 70 A.D. There is no temple today, nearly two thousand years later, but the temple will be rebuilt.

Who are these two prophets? Some would identify them by the miracles they perform. One had the power to shut up the sky so that it would not rain. That could be Elijah. The other had the power to turn water into blood. That could be Moses. Elijah and Moses were the two prophets who met Jesus on the Mount of Transfiguration. Others identify the prophets of Revelation eleven as Enoch and Elijah because those two men were gloriously taken up to heaven in their lifetime and never died. The Scripture says that "It is appointed unto men that <u>all</u> should die and after that the judgment." Still others firmly believe that one of the witnesses is John the Baptist. I do not know who they were, but I do know what happened to them.

At the end of the 1260 days of their preaching, the beast that came out of the abyss, the false prophet, put them to death. Their execution will take place at the end of the Tribulation, shortly before the coming of Christ.

By mid Tribulation Babylon had fallen. Rome was rubble. The church of the false prophet had been destroyed, but not the false prophet. He left Rome and appeared in Jerusalem for his final atrocity, the execution of God's two witnesses.

The wording of 11:8 leads me to believe that these two witnesses were crucified "...Where <u>also</u> their Lord was crucified." Unlike their Lord, they were not buried. The authorities left their bodies lying on a street in Jerusalem where for three days the people from every tribe and language and nation could gaze upon them. How could their bodies be seen throughout the entire world? Twenty- five years ago such a thing would not have been possible. However, in our day a child understands that through satellite television such a modern miracle is an ordinary occurrence.

Note in 11:10 how the world will celebrate the death of those two prophets who had stood alone witnessing for three and a half years to a world blinded by and controlled by Satan. We traditionally give gifts to celebrate a birthdate, but the world will exchange gifts to celebrate the deathdate of these two mighty prophets. How strange are the cults of Satan?

Their death is not the end of the story. These were two tremendous witnesses who served a mighty God whose power will be demonstrated three days after they die. Read what happens in verse eleven of chapter eleven. Even in the midst of this macabre scene, God shows us another bright side of the apocalypse.

People of all nations around the world will celebrate the death of those two agents of God. Floodlights will bathe their corpses and television cameras record the morbid scene day and night for worldwide broadcast. It is no wonder that great fear fell upon those who watched those two preachers come back to life three and a half days after their death The two prophets stand to their feet, dust the dirt of that Palestine street from their clothes and look up to heaven in response to a mighty voice that tells them "Come up hither." There, in view of the television cameras, the two men of God slowly ascend into the clouds just as Jesus had done 2000 years before. The Word says their enemies watched them go.

No sooner were these two men out of sight before an earthquake rocks the city of Jerusalem laying flat one out of every ten buildings and killing seven thousand people. The Word says that the people who were witnessing and experiencing these strange events finally recognized the mighty hand of God and gave Him glory.

That strange and profound story is the final event on earth before the Second Coming of Christ. Elijah and his companion arrive in heaven in time to participate in a grand worship service before the return of Christ. Jesus Christ the Mighty Conqueror mounts His white horse ready to lead the millions of His saints back to earth. I am sure these two witnesses, whether they be Moses and Elijah, or Enoch and Elijah, say, "Wait for us. We're going with you."

So we come to the sounding of the seventh and last trumpet and the seventh and last bowl -- the return of Christ to earth with His saints.

THE BRIGHT SIDE OF THE APOCALYPSE

LESSON XV

<table>
<tr><td>

DIVISION THREE

The Seventh Trumpet

Chapter 11

</td></tr>
<tr><td>

DIVISION FOUR

The Seventh Bowl

Chapter 16

</td></tr>
</table>

REVELATION CHAPTERS ELEVEN AND SIXTEEN

Revelation 11:14-19
The Seventh Trumpet/Bowl
The Prelude to the Return of Christ

The seven years of the Tribulation have ended. You and I and all the saints are in heaven. We are waiting for the signal for us to return to earth with the One known as the King of kings and the Lord of lords. The kingdoms of this world are about to become the kingdoms of our God and His Christ, and He shall reign forever and ever. (11:15.)

In chapter eleven we read of the final worship service in heaven just before the return of Christ. It is not the last such service. I am sure there will be many others after we get to heaven. Unlike the previous services which were always directed by angels, this service is led by the twenty-four elders who represent the spiritual leadership of the Old and New Testaments. The reason is this service is something special. It is the send off rally for the return of Christ. There is nothing sad or morbid about it. It will be like a giant spiritual pep rally; a service of great rejoicing. And you and I will be in that joyful crowd. All will have to admit then that the apocalypse does have a bright side.

That worship service will be held outside the temple of God in heaven. The tabernacle that Moses built in the wilderness was an exact replica of this heavenly temple. Paul talks of this in the eighth chapter Hebrews. Something about that temple is a startling verification of what I have been teaching concerning the idea that the trumpet and the bowls are the same plagues -- they occur simultaneously. Look at chapter fifteen, four chapters ahead of where we are now studying. In Revelation 15:8 the temple in heaven was shut "...And no man was able to enter the temple until the seven plagues of the seven angels were fulfilled." This statement is made before the first angel pours out his vial. Now look at 11:19 -- "The temple of God was opened in heaven." This takes place at the sounding of the seventh and final trumpet and the seventh and final bowl. As we explained, there are only seven plagues (15:8) The scene of the trumpets takes place in heaven and the scene of the bowls on earth. A comparison of these two verses in chapters fifteen and eleven can only conclude that we are correct in this key to interpretation. The temple in heaven is closed in 15:8 before the first angel turns loose his plague and is opened again in 11:19 after the seventh and last angel sounds his trumpet announcing the return of Christ.

You will find another confirmation that we are right in this reasoning in Revelations 11:19. "The lightnings, and the voices, and the thunderings, and the earthquakes, and the great hail" are exactly what are described by John in greater detail in chapter sixteen. In heaven they were aware of these activities on earth, but when John is standing on earth he can feel the impact of that great earthquake as it cuts down mountains, levels cities, and causes islands to disappear. What he describes from heaven as "great hail" on earth he can tell you how big those hailstones actually were.

These subtle insignificant observations that John records are such a blessing to me, because they confirm what I have been teaching for twenty-five years as a key principle of interpretation to the Book of Revelation. I have no right to propound a new theory of interpretation so radically different from the mainstream of Bible scholars unless the Scriptures confirm it. Praise the Lord, the Scriptures do. Others simply have not seen it.

Before we go on to chapter sixteen to observe with John what happens on earth at the sounding of the seventh trumpet, I want us to look briefly into that temple and see what is inside. It contains the ark of the covenant. This is the same ark that was so carefully placed in the holy of holies by Moses. It is now in heaven. The so-called "lost ark" is really not lost. It is not hidden in some mysterious cave or secret vault on earth. The ark rests in the temple of God in heaven. This ark is evidence of God's eternal covenant with His people the Jewish nation.

Revelation 16:17-21
The Seventh Bowl

We go now to chapter sixteen and take up the story. We are on earth with John. The last bowl is about to be poured out. I think it will be worthwhile to briefly summarize what has happened during the final three and a half years of the Tribulation.

The first four trumpet/bowls released powers and actions directed to purge planet Earth from the effects of the curse of Genesis 3:17-19 and to restore the ecology and climate of our planet to the paradise it was at the time of creation. Since I am not a scientist, I cannot even imagine how the laws of physics will be employed to effect the incredible changes depicted by John. It will not take millions of years for God to accomplish it. This tremendous renovation will be completed in less than three years. The searing heat of the sun will suck up hundreds of millions of tons of water which will form a protective water vapor in the heavens. The climate of the earth will be changed to a tropical temperature over the entire face of the earth, including the polar regions. The entire planet had burned, but already it had begun to reproduce itself with a totally new species of vegetation. God was preparing this planet Earth for the return of Christ and His people.

The world had been changed, but the people who live on earth were unchanged. The world's population will be reduced to a few million. They will refuse to repent. They will persist in their sins of idolatry, fornication and violence.When the final trumpet sounds the armies of the world will be engaged in a final climactic battle in southern Lebanon. Two hundred million men who marched from China will be locked in a bloody war with an equally great army of Europe and her allies. The battle will last for thirteen months. The toll of human life will be unbelievable. Millions will be slaughtered.

It is towards the end of that war, the "Battle of Armageddon," that the seventh angel sounds his trumpet and pours out his bowl. The result is a powerful earthquake that shudders the entire planet. There had already been cataclysmic changes on the surface of the earth caused by the impact of the two meteors. The continents have shifted and phenomenal changes have occurred in the distribution of the world's seas and oceans. With the movement of the continental plates it is not inconceivable that an earthquake of such magnitude would result.

The Word says, "There has been no such earthquake since men have been upon earth; so mighty a quake, and so great." There is no seismograph built capable of measuring this quake on the Richter scale. The city of Jerusalem will be divided into three parts. Entire cities of the world will be reduced to rubble.

John says in Revelation 16:20 that every island fled away. The Hawaiian Islands and most other islands are mountain peaks protruding from the sea. These islands will disappear because every mountain will be made low. What happened at Mount St. Helens was only a snap of God's finger compared to this event. These are the final touches to restore planet Earth to the physical condition God designed. This is the last stroke of God's power to prepare this world as a home for His people. It will be a perfect, ideal home free from every blight of sin.

God is very angry with what sin has done to His creation. In his wrath he will cause great hail stones to plummet to earth. John was there and told us that they weighed as much as a hundred pounds. Have you ever seen a hundred pound block of ice? Can you imagine the havoc such a storm would cause? How do you suppose the people on earth would react? They only respond with blasphemies against their Creator.

At this point in chapters eleven and sixteen

John brings us to the awesome moment when Jesus Christ the King of kings and the Lord of lords splits the skies and returns to Earth to restore His kingdom. That story continues in chapter nineteen. We have already completed our study of chapters seventeen and eighteen as parallel chapters to Divisions Three and Four.

THE BRIGHT SIDE OF THE APOCALYPSE

LESSON XVI

DIVISION SIX

Armageddon and the return of Jesus Christ

Chapter 19

REVELATION CHAPTER NINETEEN

Revelation 19:1-9
The Worship Service Continues in Heaven

The worship service described by John in 19:1-9 is the continuation of the service we just looked at in chapter eleven. It begins after the sounding of the final trumpet and the pouring out of the seventh bowl. The result will be an earthquake of a magnitude never felt on earth before.

In heaven the temple was opened as we saw in 11:19 and God's people gathered around the throne for a great service of praise and rejoicing. In heaven no one need be in a hurry to go home. No one will be bored of worship and praise. As the great hymn of the church says, "When we've been there ten thousand years...we'll have no less days to sing God's praise than when we first begun."

This praise service that we join in 19:1 has been going on for considerable time. It is a glorious celebration. You and I are there joining in the hallelujahs and shouts of glory and praise to the Lord. John said we sounded as the roar of many waters and the voice of mighty thunders.I have participated in some moments of jubilant ecstasy in campmeetings and revivals here on earth, but I don't think they can compare with what John is describing in this chapter. Alleluia, for the Lord God omnipotent reigneth. (19:6) The eternal battle of right against wrong is over. The victory is secured. The saints and angels are rejoicing around the throne of God. The marriage supper of the Lamb is being prepared.

For many years I was taught through sermons and in Bible School and Seminary that the "marriage supper of the Lamb" was the seven years that the saints were in heaven while the Tribulation was taking place on earth. That is not true. The Lord, as well as His saints, will be far too busy involved in the expulsion of Satan from the earth to be having any kind of a party in heaven. The marriage feast will take place when the victory has been completed. I believe that Jesus was referring to this wedding feast when He told the disciples at the Last Supper in Matthew 26:29 that He would not drink wine again until, the day that He drank it anew with His disciples in His Father's kingdom. His "Father's kingdom" is the thousand year reign of Christ on earth. The marriage supper of the Lamb will take place on earth at the beginning of the millennial kingdom.

Revelation 19:10
The Angel - John's Escort

A curious thing occurs in verse 10. John falls at the feet of the angel who has been his guide and escort through all of this fantastic revelation. The angel says to him, "Do not do it. I am a fellowservant with you..." Evidently this was no angel. It was probably one of the apostles and John had not yet recognized him as a human being in his immortal body. He certainly did not recognize him as a close associate and fellow apostle. I am sure we will recognize our loved ones in heaven. Yet it may take some time before my friends who knew me on earth will recognize me in heaven. I will no longer wear glasses. I will no longer be baldheaded, and will probably be sixty pounds lighter. I am sure when some of my friends first see me in heaven they will ask "Is that you, Harry? I thought that was you."

Revelation 19:11-16   The King is Coming

Never in the history of mankind has there been such an exciting event as that described in this section of chapter nineteen of Revelation. This is the long-awaited Second Coming of Christ. I can almost see myself there in heaven with that enormous crowd of believers that will number in the multiplied millions. They are from every corner of the globe. They are the faithful from every generation since the time of Adam. The atmosphere is electric with exuberance. The worship service has ended and preparation is being made for us to return to earth with Christ. We are awaiting that precise instant of our departure. We are destined to take literal possession of the world. It can now be said "The kingdoms of this world have become the kingdoms of our Lord." That was the theme of the song sung by the saints in the worship service in 11:15. This is that for which the church has prayed for 2000 years, "Thy kingdom come, Thy will be done, on earth as it is in heaven." Chapter nineteen ushers in the kingdom age.The glorious moment has arrived. This is the scene that had been revealed in visions and dreams to Ezekiel, Isaiah, Jeremiah, Zechariah thousands of years before. The saints of all ages have lived in expectation of this glorious day, the coming of our Saviour as King of kings and Lord of lords. Jesus Christ, the mighty conqueror, is about to return to earth. We see him at the parapet of heaven mounted on a white horse. How different is His coming now than the humble unobtrusive way He came as a babe in the manger of Bethlehem. This is not the Lamb of God. This is the Lion of the tribe of Judah He is coming to judge and make war.

The armies of the world are pitched in a final and infamous battle that has lasted for thirteen horrendous months. Millions have died in the slaughter. There has been neither time nor place to bury the dead. The world empire of Antichrist is about to crumble. He had first turned his troops against the false prophet and made war against the church. That war had lasted five months and had left his capital city of Rome a heap of charred rubble. Then the massive armies of the Orient, 200 million strong, had marched across Pakistan, India, Iran and Iraq toward this final conflagration in Palestine. The Antichrist had recruited armies from every ally he could count on to stop this pernicious invasion from China.

I am convinced that what they fought was a conventional war without any intervention of nuclear arms. It was a terrible war, but not one of world wide destruction. The struggle was concentrated in one area -- the plains of Meggai in Palestine in what is now southern Lebanon. It was a relentless battle -- a battle for survival, not of conquest.

Yet neither army was destined to survive. They were to be conquered and destroyed by a Mighty Conqueror far more powerful than the forces of Satan and the armies of all mankind. That confrontation is about to take place. Christ appears on the scene with a new and totally different army. This army does not rumble over the deserts of Lebanon in tanks and trucks. Their Commander rides a white horse. The first glimpse the people on earth will have of Him will be as He breaks through the clouds with all His saints. (Zechariah 14:5) a multitude of countless millions. "And every eye shall see him" (Revelation 1:7) This is not a secret coming as was His coming in the Rapture seven years previous. This is a glorious coming.

Have you ever wondered how it would be possible for every eye to see Him at His coming? He will set foot down on the Mount of Olives in Jerusalem and that mountain will split in two, but every eye will not witness that scene. This will not be a television event pre-announced to the media so they could be there with network cameras.

I would like to tell you how I think it will be. I believe that when Jesus Christ makes His triumphal entry to take possession of this planet Earth that He will do so in a mighty and majestic manner. I admit that this is pure speculation but it certainly could happen the way I describe it. Before He sets foot on the Mount of Olives, Jesus Christ will circle this globe orbit after orbit with his entourage of millions of saints in their glorified bodies. I believe He will split the eastern sky and sweep across the continent of Europe and the British Isles to Greenland, Iceland, New Foundland and Canada. He will cross the Aleutians to China, Tibet and Russia. Again He will circle the world on another trajectory so that the People of the United States, Japan and Korea and the midbelt of China will see the coming of the Lord and his saints. Time after time we will circle the globe. I say "we" because you and I will be in that entourage of saints. It will be a glorious day. This is what is called "The Day of the Lord." It will be **HIS** day. Before that day is over every person on five continents will have seen the glorious Son of God returning in triumph as KING OF KING AND LORD OF LORDS. How I want to be in that number.

Revelation 19:17-19
The Beast Battles Christ

A strange thing will happen in Revelation

19:19. For thirteen months the armies of Antichrist and those of the Orient were locked in a relentless death struggle.When Jesus Christ appears on the scene, the war stops.Those two armies join forces to form a common front against the Lord Almighty.

God has an army of saints, but Jesus Christ does not need us to defend His cause. You and I will be merely spectators of this event. The instant Christ's feet touch the dry parched soil of the Mount of Olives, it is obvious that this is no common Conqueror. This is the Omnipotent Son of God. That sacred mountain splits in two to demonstrate His omnipotence. (Zecharaiah 14:4) Fearlessly our Lord marches alone into battle while we His saints and followers look on in awe and amazement.

In the description that John gives us of that scene we are dressed in clean white linen while Jesus is wearing "vestures dipped in blood." It is stained with the blood of His enemies. The prophet Isaiah saw a vision in his day and asked,

Who is this which comes from Edom with his garments of crimson from Bozrah? ....Why is your apparel red and your garments like one who treads the winepress?

The Lord answered Isaiah,

I have trodden the winepress alone, and of the people there was none with me. I will find them in my anger, and triumph over them in my fury; and their blood shall be sprinkled upon my garments, and I will stain all my raiment. For the day of the vengance is in my heart, and the year of the redeemed is come

Isaiah 63:1-4

Revelation 19:20, 21
The Victory is the Lord's

The battle will be of short duration. Zechariah says that it will last one day and at the end of that day, at evening time, it shall be light. (Zech 14:7) The first beast, Antichrist, and the second beast, the false prophet, are taken captive and both are cast into the Lake of Fire burning with brimstone. (19:20) The remnant of the armies will be slain utterly that day by the sword of the Lord. Not one will escape. In a preview of this scene in Revelation 14:20 we are told, "The blood came out of the winepress even unto the horses bridles by the space of a thousand six hundred furlongs," which is about 180 miles.

There are Bible teachers who will tell you that Jesus Christ will put to death the entire population of sinners living on earth and that the earth will then be populated only by the redeemed of the Lord for the next 1000 years. That is not so. The remnant it speaks of that will be slain by the sword (19:21) is the remnant of the army, and not the entire population of the earth. We are about to enter the millennium. Clearly there will be a rebellious sinner population living on earth during those 1000 years.

THE MILLENNIUM! This certainly is the most exciting part of this study. What will the earth be like when we come back to live here? The planet will have gone through tremendous ecological changes. The climate will be tropical and very pleasant. There will be no curse of sin -- no weeds, no thorns, no blight whatsoever. It will be a totally different world.

The civilizations of this world will be in ruins. The cities of the world will be in rubble. The industries of the world will be nonexistent. Our task will be to rebuild this planet and that is what the 1000 years of the millennium is all about. To me it is tremendously exciting to contemplate what God has in store for His people.

Talk about the bright side of the apocalypse. This is it. You can count on one thing. It will be glorious, beautiful, fantastic, incredible, exciting.

There are no adjectives to describe adequately the things which God has prepared for those who love Him. Since it is true, that "Eye hath not seen, nor ear heard, neither hath it entered into the heart of man the things that God hath prepared for those who love Him" I need not be afraid to allow my imagination free reign as we attempt to discover what life will be like here on earth in the kingdom of our Lord Jesus Christ.

THE BRIGHT SIDE OF THE APOCALYPSE

LESSON XVII

DIVISION SIX

The Millennium and the White Throne Judgment

Chapter 20

REVELATION CHAPTER TWENTY

The Plan of Redemption is in Three Phases

PHASE I is the redemption of the soul, which takes place at conversion. "We who were dead in trespasses and sin have been made alive in Christ." "To us has been given the power to become the children of God." "Beloved now are we the sons of God." This is how the Scriptures express Phase I.

PHASE II is the redemption of our body.This will take place at the Rapture when those who died in Christ will be resurrected from the dead, and we who are still living at that instant of the Rapture will be caught up to meet them in the air. Paul says that at that moment we shall be changed. "This mortal will put on immortality." Our body will be redeemed, changed into a spiritual body. In our study of the Millennium we are going to see what kind of society we will build to suit that kind of body. To me it raises many pertinent and interesting questions. What kind of home will we live in? Will we need to eat and sleep? What changes will there be in work, travel and school? What about family? Will there be children in that society?

PHASE III is the redemption of this planet Earth. The Bible does not teach us that the Rapture is the end of the world. It does not teach that the Second Coming is the end of the world. It does not say that the end of the millennium will be the end of the world. When Peter says that we are looking forward to a new heaven and a new earth, the home of righteousness, he is not talking of the creation of a new planet Earth, nor of a new heaven the abode of God.

When John says in Revelation 21:1 that he saw a "new heaven and a new earth, for the first heaven and first earth had passed away" he uses almost the identical wording of II Corinthians 3:17 where Paul speaks of Phase I, the redemption of the soul. "Therefore, if any man be in Christ Jesus he is a new creature, old things are passed away, behold all things become new." These verses are not speaking of an act of creation, but one of redemption. Jesus said in Revelation 21:5 "Behold I make all things new." At the beginning of the millennium the heavens had already been restored and made new. That was not the third heaven, the abode of God; but the first heaven, our planet's atmosphere. When John describes this new earth, it had already been made new, totally renovated, totally restored.

This is one of the most thrilling revelations to be found in the Scriptures, yet most Bible scholars have missed what the Lord is saying to us. The seven years of the Tribulation and the thousand years of the millennium are for redemption, the complete restoration of this planet Earth. God has no intention to destroy this world, nor will He allow any foolish world leader under satanic direction to do so. Our God is in control. He is the sovereign Lord. We saw God's intervention when Jesus Christ took that scroll in chapter five. It was the title deed to possession of planet Earth. He has broken the seals and made good His claim to ownership. All of this drama is for a purpose. Christ does not press His claim to possession of this globe to turn around and destroy it once it is His. Nor does He intend to carry us off to some new planet in some distant

galaxy to live. "The meek shall inherit the earth"--
this earth -- this planet Earth.

What will our inheritance be like when we
come back to reclaim it? Maybe we could compare
this "new earth" to the planet as it was at
creation. We know something about the garden of
Eden. Beautiful, magnificent, stupendous are the
adjectives we would have to use to describe it if we
had seen its splendor. God described the work of
His creation in one simple word -- "He saw that it
was GOOD." It pleased Him It was perfect. The
world we come back to will be no less perfect.The
earth is to be redeemed. God's design is to provide
a marvelous place where we will live.

Food will grow profusely. Adam had no need
to cultivate the soil. As it was then, so it will be in
our future world. There will be no weeds, no
thorns, no blight, no decay, no harmful parasites.
The climate of the entire globe will be
semitropical, including the polar regions. There
will be no massive deserts, no barren land, no
wasteland. Every square foot of the earth's surface
will be productive and inhabitable. There was no
rain before the great flood. Likewise, there will be
no rain on the new earth. There will be no floods,
no erosion. The earth will be amply watered by
mist and dew. Remember, the entire planet will
once again be enshrouded with a great clear vapor

that was called in Genesis 1:8 the firmament. The atmosphere will have been cleansed from all pollution and restored to the ideal balance of elements as God designed it to be. The vapor shroud around the globe will not only provide an ideal climate, but it will also protect the surface of the earth from the sun's harmful radiation and ultra violet rays. The climate on earth will be absolutely ideal.

Never again will there ever be a starving child with a distended stomach and spindly limbs dying for lack of an adequate diet. There will be no hunger on earth, no tuberculosis, no rickets, no malnutrition. There will be an abundant supply of food for everyone everywhere. When the new plant life breaks through the ashes of the fire that burned up a third of the forests midway in the Tribulation, new exotic fruits and vegetables will sprout that you and I have never savored. We are talking about the bright side of the apocalypse. As I have said numerous times, the meaning of apocalypse is the end of evil. Every effect of sin and the curse of sin will be wiped away. What does that mean?

Does it mean that there will be no more sickness, no more disease, no more death? Not quite. For us who will return to earth in our immortal spiritual bodies, yes -- absolutely yes. However, we will not be the only people living on earth during the millennium. Millions of unsaved inhabitants of earth will miraculously survive the earthquakes, firestorms and war of the seven years of Tribulation. They will co-habitate the planet along with the redeemed saints. In addition, children will be born to those people during the millennium. Their number will multiply incredibly over that span of a thousand years.

These people are still mortals. They bring with them into the millennium the sicknesses and diseases they harbor in their bodies. However, the Bible says of the children born during the kingdom age that a person will still be a child at 100 years of age. Will he be a hundred year old infant? No, that is not what the prophecy means. It does mean that the mortal inhabitants of this planet will have a greatly extended life span, much like earth's early inhabitants in the Old Testament. Methusala lived 969 years. Lamech lived 777 years. Noah lived 950 years. Others died much sooner, and so it will be in the millennium. How will we live side by side - - mortals with immortals? How will such a society be governed? What will such a world be like?

The planet itself will be completely restored and ready for habitation when we return to earth with Christ to begin the millennial reign. However, the works of man will be in shambles. Cities will have been reduced to rubble. Every industry, and all communications, and transportation will have to be totally rebuilt. What a challenge, what an opportunity to rebuild our world without the flaws that plague our society today.

Sociologists have written countless books and dissertations describing what to them would be the ideal society. It is not difficult to identify the ills of our present society, and I assume that those ills will be remedied in that new society. We are told that if we are ever going to have peace and justice on this earth, we must obliterate all national boundaries, monetary systems, passports, and closed societies. We must make our people "world citizens" with total freedom to visit or live where they choose. We will not be citizens of a country. We will be citizens of the world. The problems of the world are not national. They are global. Problems such as economic depression, terrorism, disease, pollution, famine unshared resources, weather modification, food distribution, communication, and transportation are all global projects according to modern sociologists. "Our problems will never be resolved on a nationalistic basis," say these sociologists. Our awareness of these problems is becoming increasingly universal. The solution is one universal government -- one universal citizenship.

Undoubtedly the sociologists, economists, scientists and diplomats are right in their suggested solution. Their problem is how to achieve one universal government, because we live in a world governed by the law of the jungle -- survival of the fittest. Those who dominate and govern us are not necessarily the best and wisest. They are simply the most powerful. Man in his fallen, sinful egotistical state is incapable of governing the world. Neither Marxism, humanism, capitalism nor socialism will ever achieve this idealistic goal of one universal government.

Who would be capable of being the head of such a government? What system of government would it be? How would that person achieve that position of world power? Do you know that all these questions are answered in the Book of Revelation?

There is only one person who is pure enough, wise enough, righteous enough and powerful enough to be that ideal universal world leader. His name is Jesus Christ, Son of God, Son of man. It is He who will set up a world government here on earth. He himself will be the monarch, the king, the ultimate authority. The government He will form will be neither democracy nor dictatorship. It will be a monarchy. His title will be King. His kingdom will be the world. He will rule over every tribe and nation in every corner of all five continents.

There will be no more national boundaries. We will not be citizens of the United States or Japan or Great Britain. We will be world citizens. What the League of Nations, the United Nations, and scores of powerful dictators have never accomplished, Jesus Christ will achieve. His kingdom will be one universal world government. The resources of the world will belong to everyone. There will be no more third world nations. The beauty of the world will belong to everyone.There will be no restrictions as to where anyone chooses to live. There will be no passports, no visas, no closed societies, no poverty, no hatred, no war. We will see what the world will be like when we see righteousness and justice reign.

This idea of an open society under a universal world government sounds good, but it will not happen all at once. We will have to make it happen. I look at the millennium as 1000 years of reconstruction in which you and I will definitely be involved. We are not going to sit around for a thousand years doing nothing as some people have taught.

Can you visualize the world we will be coming back to? Have you added up all the devastation of the last three and a half years of the Tribulation brought about by wars, earthquakes, firestorms and tidal waves? Can you visualize what the Word means when it implies that all the coastal plains of all the continents will be completely washed away? All the costal cities will be wiped out -- San Diego, Los Angeles, Santa Barbara, San Francisco, Portland, Bremmerton, Seattle, Boston, New York, Norfolk, Charleston, Fort Lauderdale, Miami, Tampa, New Orleans, Galveston -- to name a few in the United States. Add to that list Tokyo, Singapore, Honolulu, Lima, Valparaiso, Buenos Aires and scores of other oceanside cities worldwide. When the polar axis of this world is changed, the resulting tidal waves will dwarf any tsunami ever recorded in history -- and that upheaval will be worldwide. Did you sense the impact of the words in Revelation, "The cities of the world were destroyed."

The earthquake described as being more powerful than any in all history since the creation of man is going to level every city. There isn't a skyscraper built that will withstand those tremors. Every one of those buildings will be reduced to rubble. During the few years that remain in the Tribulation after the earthquake no one will even attempt to rebuild them.

It is curious to me, in the light of this

terrible desolation, that this is not a problem. It is the solution. Sociologists tell us that we must rid our planet of obsolete, old world cities if we are ever going to have a world conducive to peace, prosperity, health and happiness. The crowded, cockroach infested tenements, the sunless streets, the bleak factory buildings, the decaying neighborhoods must all go. Los Angeles, San Francisco, Chicago, New York, London, Tokyo -- all must go.

They are right. However, no one has any workable plan to even begin such worldwide urban renewal. God does. When we come back to this planet to live we will be given the tremendous task of rebuilding the cities of the world.

What kind of cities will they be? Do you suppose we are going to reconstruct crowded tenement buildings, drab factories, dismal ghettos? I don't think so. The cities we build will be designed to accommodate a totally different lifestyle. In the Kingdom Age you can expect to live a totally different life from what we are living now. Our values will not be in what we own, but in who we are and in what we do. We will be world citizens. There will be so much to do and so much to see that the least of our ambitions will be to accumulate wealth and possessions.

Our principle possession in our present

society is our home. We invest all our resources in that property, in that building and in its furnishings. The home of the future will be far less fixed and far more mobile. It will not be built of stone, brick, steel and concrete. It will not be built for permanence. We will not be a rooted society. Nothing will be built to get old, to decay and degenerate into ghettoes.

Think of an ideal community, in an ideal setting in an ideal place, an ideal size and you will begin to conceive what those cities will look like. I don't suppose that any of those communities will be larger than 50,000 to 100,000 people. There will be no more cities of eight and nine million like Buenos Aires and Tokyo.

We are going to see so many changes in family, work and travel that such cities would be totally inappropriate to our needs. These new cities will combine the most beautiful aspects of nature with the latest technology to suit our new and liberated life style.

This won't be heaven, but it will be like heaven on earth. It will be the sociologist's dream. This is the new world that has been promised to us. Do you recall the parable of the talents where the man who had doubled his five talents was given his reward -- "You will be ruler over ten cities." These are the kind of cities that were promised to him. They will be beautiful.

Another beautiful development in our new life concerns our work habits. Surprisingly, the economists and sociologists who describe the ideal society tell us that we must get rid of the work ethnic built into our society and the guilt we feel about unemployment and leisure time. The compulsion to work is ingrained in our society. Zero unemployment is the ideal for our economy. We have forgotten that part of the curse of sin was that man would live by the sweat of his brow. We have given work a puritan value. Hardship and hard work are good for you. "Idle hands are the devil's workshop." That attitude has to change.

No society is free until we are released from the slavery of our jobs and careers and the endless struggle for survival. In the ideal society there will be more leisure and less work; more enjoyment, and less hardship. We must have more time to give us the freedom to travel, to learn, to spend time with friends and family. We must have time and opportunity to get acquainted with and be a part of the world in which we live. I sit here and dream of all the places I would like to go, and of all the things I would like to do, but there has never been time or opportunity to do them.

I am sure we will work during the millennium. I certainly hope so. Evidently there will be plenty of work to do, but our work will be very different. I can imagine working two days a week with five days to call our own; or a schedule of working three months with nine months to invest in other interests.

Another of the ancient institutions of our society that is being attacked by sociologists as being obsolete and no longer necessary, is the traditional family. Little by little we see the erosion of family life in our society. The so called nuclear family of father, mother and children has replaced the extended family of a generation ago. We care for our elderly in institutions. Brothers and sisters no longer receive from the family a tract of land on the corner of the farm where they build their home and raise their children in a community of aunts and uncles, brothers and sisters, mother and father -- all under the shadow of grand dad's house. Even the nuclear family is being rapidly undermined. Our children are being raised even more by single parents. The sad thing is that our government and society think that this is the direction the family should go. In reality the family no longer exists.

We are told that there is no need for the family. It is already obsolete. There is no longer any need for the family in the reproduction of children. Procreation can be done through sperm and egg banks using artificial wombs in laboratories. The genes of these children can be carefully selected and controlled by genetic scientists. The children of today's society should belong to the world, and not to any parents in particular. This is the "New Age" society projected by humanists who think they have the solution to the ills of the world as we see it today. How pathetic.

Oddly enough, we are going to see some of those drastic changes in the family during the Kingdom Age. The Book of Revelation and the entire Bible speak to this issue of the family in the future. The family was ordained by God for the replenishing of this planet. It has never become obsolete, but it will be. People talk about marriage as an eternal state. It really is not. Jesus enlightened us about the future family in one of His encounters with the Pharisees in which they made up a ridiculous situation to entrap Jesus. Under Jewish law, when a man married a woman, and then died before bearing any children; his brother had to marry the widow and bear children with her so as to carry on his name. The Pharisees made up a situation in which a woman had married seven brothers and each time her husband died before she had any children. "In the resurrection", they asked of Jesus, "Whose wife shall she be of the seven?" They envisioned seven husbands fighting over this one woman when they all got to heaven. Jesus answered, "Ye do err, not knowing the Scriptures.... for in the resurrection" he said, "they neither marry, nor are given in marriage, but are as the angels of God in heaven".

The purpose of marriage is for the procreation and care of children. The best environment for raising children is the family. Obviously there will be no children born to the saints during the Kingdom Age and throughout eternity and consequently there will be no need for the family as we know it in our society today.

Then what relationship will we have between sexes? It will be a deep, glorious, beautiful relationship of love but not of marriage and family. We will probably have very close and loving relationships with many people. The Bible does not say that we will be sexless, and I do not know what role sex will play in our relationships. Whatever it is, it will be pure and holy.

What about children? What about the millions of infants who have died and gone to heaven? What will be their state in the millennium? How old will they be? I believe that if we asked Jesus these questions He would answer just as He did the Pharisees in their question concerning marriage. "...They will be as the angels of God in heaven." That simple statement opens up to me glorious possibilities for the remedy of one of our society's most serious problems.

A serious injustice of our society is that we are not created equal in spite of Abraham Lincoln's declaration. The handsome prince will carry away the beautiful peasant girl on his white stallion. But what of the fat, ugly girl that nobody falls in love with? The tall, handsome, virile athlete will be the hero of our society. What of the weaklings, the sickly, the crippled, the less fortunate? Where is justice and equality when I am confined to a body that cannot be changed to my liking and to my needs? If I am black I just have to accept that I am black. If I am short I just have to accept that I am short. There is little I can do to correct these predestined inequalities of my life. The sociologists have no satisfactory solution for these inequalities and injustices that are "accidents of birth". However, the Lord does have a solution. If we are to be as the angels, then we should study the characteristics of angels to determine what we will be like.

Apparently an angel is capable of taking on any form he chooses. The angels who appeared to Abraham looked and talked like the people of Abraham's day. When an angel appeared to the parents of Samson they could not distinguish him from a man in their day. This characteristic of our spiritual body to be able to assume different forms is confirmed by Jesus on the road to Emmaus. Luke tells us that "He took another form" and for that reason was not recognized by those two disciples.

If we are going to be like angels, we will be able to choose whatever age and body form we might desire. You may choose to live with blacks in Africa and prefer to be black; or with orientals in China and blend in with their culture. Do not expect that the God who makes every snowflake, every blade of grass, every leaf, and every cloud different from all others is going to mold us into one color, one race, one age, one style? No, my friend. If anything, there will be more variety -- endless variety. But there will be no inequality. Those ills of our present society will be remedied by the simple fact that we will be like the angels.

Another important thing about angels is that they are eternal beings. They can assume the aspect of any age, but they themselves never age. Gabriel is no older today than he was when he appeared to the Virgin Mary. They never grow old. They never die. Time has no effect on them.

Time is probably one of the most insidious

enemies of life. It is eating up our life. Time is the stuff life is made of. Time is running out, and I must run with it, for my life is running out.We keep hoping that it will not run out before we are through. It seems like the longer we live, the faster time goes.There is so much to be done and so little time in which to do it.There is no time for family. There is no time for friends. There is no time for leisure.There is no time to get our work done.We never catch up.This time-tension is a race to the finish.The more we try to accomplish the more futile it seems.

This is another dilemma of our society about which sociologists can do very little. Not so with the Lord. He has already taken care of the problem. The day is coming when we will hear Him say, "Time will be no more." It will take some getting used to having all the time to get done all that we would like to do. When time ceases, so will the pressures of competition and stress cease. We will no longer be compelled to run. The rat race will be over. Why run? We will have all the time we need to accomplish all of our goals and ambitions. It will never be late.

Humankind has another tremendous dilemma related to time, our mortality. Every day I am a little older, a little weaker, a little closer to the grave. The process of death sets in the day we are born. Life is a continual struggle against disease, infection, infirmities and decay. When our bodies can no longer put up a fight, we die. We do our best to patch things. We replace our teeth as they fall out. We strengthen our faulty vision with eye glasses. We implant pacemakers and replace failing organs -- all in a futile effort to add a few more meaningful years to our life. Ultimately it is appointed unto man to die. We are mortal. Miracle drugs may prolong our life a few more days or at the most a few more years, but death is inevitable.

How can society go anywhere when every human being lives on the verge of death? None of us are certain of another fifteen minutes. We can choke on a grape. We can drown in a spoonful of water. We could step off the curb in front of a speeding car. There is no way that we can protect ourselves from our exposure to death. No matter how bright or how promising might be our future, when we die it is over. At least for the humanist that is so. How sad and depressing all this must be to the atheist and humanist who deny life hereafter; how fatal, how tragic. Faced with that tragedy, man in his humanistic philosophy is attempting to discover the secret of immortality. Some think they have found it in the ancient pagan philosophy of re-incarnation. Others are confident that science will discover a way to beat the angel of death who hovers over man's life. To the humanist death is the greatest tragedy of humanity. The imminence of death and the uncertainty of life probably brings us more anxiety than all other stresses combined. Death is so final. To the humanist death is the end. There is no afterlife. There is nothing beyond. All the happiness and all the fulfillment we will ever enjoy are in this brief mortal life. How much more we could accomplish if we were immortal. God has good news for us. We are immortal. "Death has been swallowed up in victory." "I am the resurrection and the life." Jesus said, "He that believeth in me shall never die."

As if that were not enough, there is more. What God has planned for us is not simply life, simply an eternal existence. Don't ever believe that heaven consists of our sitting on a cloud playing a harp throughout an endless eternity. We will learn in this study a little of what eternity will be like. But the Word assures us, "that eye hath not seen, nor ear heard, neither hath it entered into the heart of man what the Lord hath prepared for those who love him." No matter how beautiful and glorious a picture I might paint of heaven we know that the half has never yet been told, nor ever will be told of what it will really be like.

Friend, this is no message of doom and

gloom. The apocalypse is not a tragic drama. It is the glorious account of the fantastic future every child of God will enjoy throughout eternity. When Paul wrote, "Look up, for your redemption draweth nigh," and "Comfort one another with these sayings," he was not thinking of doom and disaster. He was looking at the bright side of the apocalypse. He was showing us a plan and project designed by God for us. It is for our well being. The Revelation of Jesus Christ is the unveiling, the revealing of that plan.We are talking about a future that you can look forward to with joy and anticipation, not with fear and dread; inspite of the dismal depressing headlines of today's newspapers.What God has planned for us is so great and glorious that Jesus said, "It would be better to pluck out your eyes and go through life blind rather than miss it."

Can you imagine what kind of society we will have with such dramatic changes? This is not pie in the sky by and by. I am talking about how you and I will live right here on earth and it could be within the next seven years if Jesus Christ should return to rapture His church today. When Jesus comes back to earth, He will set up a world government. Jerusalem will probably be the world capital. The government will be a monarchy, and that form of government will filter down through every town and hamlet worldwide. Every government position will be filled by a Christian believer. The saints will be in charge.

There will be millions of unbelievers living on earth during the millennium but they will share equally in the blessings and prosperity of the rule of Christ. It will be a peaceful, happy, fulfilled society for them as well as for us, the children of God. The needs of these mortal people living on earth will be totally different from ours since they will be confined to mortal bodies while you and I will enjoy spiritual bodies. Whereas we will not need cars and busses, ships and airplanes to get from one place to another, they will. You and I will be able to move from one continent to another in an instant simply by wishing it to be so. Would you like to see that demonstrated in the Bible? After the resurrection the disciples left Jerusalem and walked the 100 miles or so to the Sea of Galilee where they met with the Lord. Jesus no longer had to walk those miles. His was a spiritual body that existed in a different dimension and conformed to different laws of physics. The Word says we will be like Him. I don't believe there were any spaceships that appeared on the hills of Bethlehem to bring the angels that sang the first Christmas carols to the shepherds announcing the birth of Jesus. They simply appeared and then returned to where they had come from. We will be like them.

We will not necessarily have to eat or sleep. It will be an option. Jesus ate fish and bread with the disciples at the breakfast he prepared for them after the resurrection at the Sea of Galilee. It wasn't because He needed the nourishment. He ate for fellowship. I like that. I enjoy pie and coffee after church not because I need the food. It is because I enjoy the fellowship.However, the rest of the inhabitants of earth will have to eat to nourish their mortal bodies. As we have already seen, food will be in abundance everywhere. There will be no need for frozen foods and preservatives. There will probably be no need for grocery stores as we know them. There will be plenty to eat and readily available for everyone everyday.

We will not have children, but the mortals will. Those children will have to be cared for and educated. I am sure that the children of the entire world will be a delight to all of us. The redeemed ones, you and I, will share in the loving care of those little ones.There will be no unwanted children, no abused children, and no unloved children in the Kingdom Age.

Revelation 20:1-3
Satan Bound a Thousand Years

The second best thing, next to being with Christ on earth, is the assurance that Satan and all his evil influence will be banned from earth for those millennial years. He will be bound and cast into the bottomless pit and shut up and sealed. Later in our study we will see that at the conclusion of the thousand years Satan will be loosed for a little while. We will see what he does and why.

Revelation 20:4-6
The Reign of the Saints

The ultimate authority during the millennium will be Jesus Christ.He will undoubtedly rule from Jerusalem. In His kingdom every place of leadership, every throne, every seat of judgment, every city council, every school board, every industry, every civic organization will be directed and controlled by the saints, the children of God. "We shall reign with Him a thousand years".(Rev. 20:6) I can very well imagine, though, that not all unbelievers will be happy with Christians running city hall and all the schools. Can you fancy how today's liberals would feel about living in a totally Christian environment. There will be no bars, no nightclubs, no drugs, no prostitution. It will be interesting to see how our unsaved neighbors will react to that situation. But whether they like it or not we will be in charge. John continually reminds us that those children of God not only include the church that was caught up in the Rapture, but also the millions of converts who were converted to Christ during the first half of the Tribulation.

Revelation 20:7-10
Satan Loosed a Little While

The dispensation of grace and forgiveness ended midpoint in the Tribulation. None of the survivors of the Tribulation who had taken the mark of the beast, nor any of their children, would ever be saved; not even the children born to them during the Kingdom Age. However, these children were still free moral agents and they had to be given the opportunity to choose their eternal destiny. For that reason Satan was loosed at the end of the thousand years. He could once again spread his lies and deceit across the face of the earth. Before the end of the 1000 year period all the mortals who had survived the Tribulation would have died. Their descendants are the ones put to this testing by Satan.

Incredible as it seems, Satan is totally successful in this diabolical endeavor. Millions of people on earth who had lived a thousand years under the rulership of Christ. They had lived side by side with millions of eternally saved saints in an ideal environment. They are now given an opportunity to choose between serving Christ or serving Satan. Every last man, woman and child of those mortals living on earth will choose to side with Satan in his final effort to overpower Jesus Christ. This attitude served to justify the judgment of God against these people. They were now eternally doomed to damnation.

Satan will organize these followers into a vast army and march on the beloved city of Jerusalem. Their efforts will be futile, however. God will simply rain fire from heaven and destroy them. This is what is going to happen. It is not symbolic, nor is it a figure of speech. This is the closing chapter in the history of mortal mankind. The last sinner will have gone to face his Maker in judgment.

Satan himself will be cast into the lake of fire and brimstone to join the false prophet and Antichrist who were already consigned to that place of eternal torment before the millennial age began. None of that trio will ever escape from that place of eternal punishment. "They will be tormented day and night forever and ever."

Revelation 20:11-15
The White Throne Judgment

The Scripture has declared for all to hear: "It is appointed unto men once to die, and after that the judgment." (Hebrews 9:27) Many have scoffed. Many have denied it. Many have taught us lies to alleviate our fears, but nothing can change the fact. "We shall all appear before the judgment seat of Christ, that everyone may receive the things done in his body, according to that he hath done, whether it be good or bad." (II Cor 5:10).

It is that final judgment that John witnesses and describes in these verses under consideration from Revelation chapter twenty. Every man, woman and child from the entire human race will be there. Adam, his wife Eve, their children and every descendant of Adam will be called to appear on that awesome day. The graves will give up their dead. The sea will give up the multiplied thousands who have died beneath its waves. It will not matter in the resurrection that those bodies have long since turned to ashes or that many were devoured by the fish of the sea. Just as every believer was resurrected bodily at the Rapture, so now every unbeliever will be called forth from his grave, given an immortal body and compelled to face the terror of God's final judgment. None will escape. None will be excused.

When Paul said that every man would stand before the judgment seat of Christ he meant all of us -- believers as well as unbelievers. The apostle Paul himself will be there to be judged. The judgment is not to determine who is to be saved and who is to be lost. That was determined the day you and I confessed Jesus Christ as Lord and accepted Him as our Saviour. If you never confessed Christ as your Saviour you will stand at the judgment lost and condemned. It will not be a matter of weighing your good deeds against the bad to determine whether you are acceptable to God. Our acceptance is based upon our relationship to Jesus Christ and the resultant fact that our names are recorded in the Lamb's Book of Life. That book will separate the sheep from the goats.

In addition to the Book of Life, John saw other books being opened. Apparently these are a written record of all of our deeds, both good and bad. In the case of the believer this judgment will determine the degree of our rewards and for the unbeliever it will determine the degree of his punishment. Obviously a just judgment must wait until all the facts are in. This judgment cannot be made in our lifetime for the influence of our lives continues on after us. It won't be until the day of judgment that the cumulative impact of our existence will be judiciously evaluated and rewarded.

That will be a fearful day for all of us. Some years ago I heard a great man of God make a frightening declaration in the closing years of his ministry. This is what he said. "Sometimes I am afraid to die for fear I have not done my very best." That man was Dr. R. T. Williams Sr., General Superintendent of the Church of the Nazarene, a preacher of holiness, a man of God, a great evangelist who had led thousands to Christ. If a man like him feared to face the judgment, what about the rest of us? Many of us will stand before the King speechless, chagrined, empty handed and embarrassed. There will be many who will manage to get through the pearly gates knowing that they barely made it.

Will there be differences of rewards for the Christians? Yes, there will be. Will heaven not be the same for all of us? No, it will not. How can that be? Will some be disappointed and unhappy in heaven? No, there will be no unhappiness in heaven for anyone. Maybe I can illustrate how I think heaven will be.

Years ago I used to attend Hollowrock Holiness Campmeeting at a campgrounds along the Ohio river a few miles from Steubenville, Ohio. When you enter the campgrounds you come upon a softball diamond and see several dozen campers joyfully playing ball. As you drive into the parking area you will notice that several people are sitting in their cars listening to the radio. Others are strolling along the pathways of the campgrounds thoroughly enjoying themselves. Along the hillside are huge dormitories and the dining hall. Each of those buildings has an ample porch and on those porches are dozens of people sitting in rocking chairs or on the steps. They are fellowshipping, conversing, reading the Bible, or just resting. As we walk on down the path towards the tabernacle we pass a number of rustic cottages. Some of these are built along the four sides of the great auditorium. From those cottages you can hear the singing and listen to the preaching while cooking dinner and washing dishes without even leaving your little cabin. The tabernacle itself seats about 1000 people. You will find people seated on the back rows as far from the platform as they can get. Others have brought their chairs and cushions and have accommodated themselves in the straw around the altar only a few feet from the fiery preaching of the fervent evangelists. These saints are about as close as they can get to enjoy the glory and blessing of campmeeting.

All of these people we have described are inside the campgrounds and all are where they want to be. Some are content to be barely inside the gate playing ball, whereas others are seated at the feet of the evangelists drinking in the spiritual blessings. All are happy. All are satisfied. Some are far more blessed than others. I think that is a good illustration of how heaven will be for you and me. However, remember this; your position in heaven will be eternally determined by the closeness of your walk with Christ here on earth. The spiritual Christian on earth will be the spiritual Saint in heaven.

Whereas every believer can anticipate a glorious reward in heaven, Revelation 20:15 tells of the horrible fate of the unbelievers. "Whoever was not found written in the Book of Life was cast into the lake of fire." The Bible says, "It is a fearful thing to fall into the hands of an angry God." This lake of fire is the final eternal hell prepared for the devil and his angels. Here we see that it is to be the eternal destination of Satan's followers as well. The words, "where they shall be tormented day and night forever and ever" is terribly frightening. There is such a finality about these words, forever and ever. The dreadful thought is that there is no finality. There is no end to this sentence. It is a torment that will never cease, never diminish.

Does all this sound like doom and gloom? The future of this world is as bright as the promises of God's Word. The tragedy is that so many thousands of people hear the Good News and yet reject that Gospel for the pleasures of sin for a season. I grant you, the sinner who rejects God's love and salvation does not have much of a future. Let me tell you something, sinner friend.

Right now you may think that God is cruel and unjust. He plans the punishment and suffering that millions of people are going to experience in Tribulation judgment. However, when you stand before God on the day of judgment and hear His verdict concerning your guilt, you will be compelled to confess that God was right and just. You rejected His Son Jesus Christ and chose your own destiny. Now is the time to make the right decision. Confess your need. Repent of your sins. Accept Jesus Christ as your personal Saviour. Do that, my friend, and you can be part of the beautiful, spectacular plan God has for you and me in that glorious future. I can assure you that one day in the kingdom of our Lord will be worth everything it might have cost you to make it.

The message of the Gospel is that God "is not willing that any should perish, but that all should come to repentance." (II Peter 3:9) Hell was not made for humankind. If you or I ever end up in that lake of fire, we will be there as a result of our own choice. We choose our destiny. It will be the lake of fire with eternal torment or our heavenly home with its eternal bliss. Chapter twenty one will give us some inkling of what that bliss will be like.

THE BRIGHT SIDE OF THE APOCALYPSE

LESSON   XVIII

DIVISION SEVEN

**The New Heaven and
the New Earth
The New Jerusalem**

Chapter 21

REVELATION CHAPTER TWENTY ONE

This chapter gives us a glimpse far into the future. It takes us beyond the millennium to the very edge of eternity. John tells of a spectacular event that seems to be taken from a space odyssey. What John describes appears to be more incredible than the imagination of today's most prolific writers of science fiction. The scene is fascinating. It is an event that will take place following the White Throne Judgment at the end of the millennium.

The thousand year reign of Christ on earth has ended. God has restored the world as a paradise for the human race. Its beauty and splendor excels that of the Garden of Eden. This new paradise will not be populated by two solitary people in a rural setting of Eden, but by a civilization of multiplied millions. None of those millions of inhabitants will be mortal human beings. We will be immortal spiritual beings but not spirits. We will have bodies that occupy space. We will have minds that think, reason and rationalize and hunger for knowledge. We will have character and personality. What we will not have is sin. The human race will have been purged of the last vestige of sin. For the first time in thousands, if not millions of years, the planet Earth as well as the entire universe will be rid of Satan, his angels, his followers, and all the evil that has blighted God's creation. Every dark and evil effect of sin will have been utterly destroyed. What can we expect next? The world has been reconstructed. The millennial reign of Christ has ended. It is with much anticipation that we open chapter twenty-one of the Book of Revelation to discover what will happen next.

Revelation 21:1
The New Heaven and the New Earth

Listen to those words of John in 21:1. "And I saw a new heaven and a new earth; for the first heaven and the first earth were passed away; and there was no more sea."

These are words spoken by John, a fisherman of the first century. He had lived to see the rise and fall of the Roman empire. He was alive in 70 AD when the city of Jerusalem was sacked, leveled and burned by Roman hordes. This John is the beloved disciple of Jesus. He had been associated with Jesus here on earth for three years. John was there on a hill called Calvary when the soldiers crucified his Lord. He believed in Jesus. He knew Him to be the Son of God. He was willing to stake his life on that belief. It was for his faith in Jesus that John was on the Island of Patmos, exiled and left to die. He knew the impact of the Gospel on the first century world. John was acquainted with the Apostle Paul who had been beheaded in Rome a few years before John recorded this Revelation. Before John died he witnessed the moral decline of the empire of the Ceasars. He grieved at the slaughter of hundreds of thousands of Christians. He saw a world that was plunging headlong into chaos and barbarianism. Those were sad and depressing days for this world called Earth.

Then from the Isle of Patmos John is catapulted 2000 years into the future. An angel escorts him through seven years of tribulation like the world has never known. He recognized the old

Roman empire revived under the satanic rule of Antichrist. He relived the scene of the persecution of the church that paled the atrocities of the first century. Millions upon millions of Christians are ruthlessly slaughtered by the Gestapo like forces of Antichrist. John had never seen such carnage in his century. He was appalled by the military hardware of a modern police state.

The worst of those weapons was unleashed midpoint in the Tribulation when a brief but devastating nuclear conflagration threatened to destroy the entire world. Russia and several other nations, including the United States of America were practically annihilated. John saw it all. Those were exceedingly dark days for this world. The only bright moment was the glorious resurrection of the millions of martyred saints midpoint in those seven ravaging years. The saints were swept into heaven, and John saw and recorded the glorious scene.

For the next three and a half years John witnessed God's tremendous unlimited power recreating the splendor of this small planet called Earth. Two stars the size of mountains nudged the planet into a new orbit and shifted the globe onto a new axis. Entire continents were moved into new positions. Great earthquakes rocked the world as the earth reeled like a drunkard. Enormous tidal waves washed across the coastal plains. Every city on earth was reduced to rubble. It looked as if an angry God was intent on destroying the world He had created.

But not so. Out of the rubble and out of the chaos sprouted lush tropical vegetation. This wasn't destruction. It was creation. John heard Jesus shout over the bedlam, "BEHOLD I MAKE ALL THINGS NEW."A new world was being formed. Paradise was being restored. This paradise was far more beautiful than the first. It was to this new world that Jesus Christ escorted His saints and lived and reigned with them 1000 years. They rebuilt a world society under the divine leadership of THE KING OF KINGS AND LORD OF LORDS.

It is all complete in the opening verse of chapter twenty-one. Modern spectacular cities have been rebuilt.There is not one charred trace of any destruction or chaos. Everything is beautiful. John looks out over the scene and describes what he saw, "A new heaven and a new earth for the first heaven and the first earth were passed away." This is redemption not creation. John spoke of the redemption of the purchased possession, the planet we call home.

I do not believe for a minute that at the end of chapter twenty our planet Earth is destroyed and we go to live in another galaxy on another planet called Earth. John is not describing a new heavenly body called Earth. He is standing right here in this world utterly astounded by the beauty of our restored redeemed world. The new heaven does not refer to heaven the abode of God, but to the atmosphere, the new firmament that is placed as a canopy around our globe. But that is only the beginning.

Revelation 21:2-9
Jesus Declares His new
Covenant With Men

John gives us an inkling of what is about to happen. He makes this majestic statement in 21:2 "I, John, saw the holy city, the new Jerusalem, coming down from God out of heaven." He will give us a detailed description of that incredible sight beginning at verse nine, but first he listens to Jesus declare His new covenant with men.

God himself, the first person of the Trinity, was coming to our world to dwell. That is a phenomenal statement. In our day the visit of the Pope to any country on earth is an occasion for great excitation. It is a media event that surpasses all others. Non Catholics as well as Catholics are aware of a sphere of power that seems to surge around that man wherever he goes. If that is true of a human being, the pontiff of an earthly religious organization, can you imagine what it will be like when God appears on earth with his monstrous tabernacle called the New Jerusalem. The famous "popemobile" pales in comparison.

In verses four through seven God declares to us the terms of the new covenant. There will be no more tears, no crying, no sorrow, no death, no pain -- ever again. How could you calculate the amount of pain and suffering the human race has experienced in our 6000 years of existence? All that is over. Jesus has promised us life, and that abundantly. God makes available to us the fountain of the water of life. You and I will freely enjoy the limitless potential of life at its fullest. We will enjoy knowledge, emotions, expressions, fulfillment beyond anything any human being has ever experienced. It is difficult to comprehend how that expansion of our existence will translate in your life and mine. It would be like an earthworm who had never been out of your back yard. Now you are going to give that worm the body and mind of a human being and the freedom to explore a world he never knew existed. There is knowledge and experience and emotions and relationships and places that we will become a part of; but in our finite state we are not aware that they even exist. I have to believe that there are other worlds that God has created. They are out there beyond our reach. Man has made pitiful attempts to explore our universe and beyond. I want to know about those worlds. I want to be there. That may not interest you at all. Your interest might be in music or flowers or birds. That could be your universe to explore and enjoy. Jesus had promised that the meek would inherit the earth, and we will. God now expands that promise in 21:7. We will not only inherit the earth but all things everywhere in every corner of this and every other universe. There is a vast unknown out there that is part of God's creation and it will be ours to know and to own.

Revelation 21:9-21
The New Jerusalem The City of God

What John described at the beginning of this chapter is the holy city, the new Jerusalem, the tabernacle of God. It will be shown in elaborate detail in these next few verses.

In verse nine an angel comes to John. It is one of those seven angels who had blown those trumpets and emptied those vials of the "seven last plagues." He escorts John to a vantage point at the top of a great and high mountain. John has a front seat view to witness what is about to take place. It is to be an awesome sight like no mortal has ever seen. The only high mountains in that vicinity of the world had to be either the Alps or the Himalayas. I personally believe that John was taken right to the top of Mt. Everest -- the roof of the world, the highest point on earth. From there the angel pointed out a bright light in the sky more brilliant than any star. That light was approaching earth; coming closer, and closer and closer.

As it grew near John identified it as a great city descending from space. As this celestial body drew closer John could begin to appreciate the awesomeness of what he saw. We would call it a satellite in our day. But what a satellite this was! No space scientist or science fiction writer ever envisioned a satellite of these enormous dimensions. We are told the size -- 1500 miles long, 1500 miles wide and 1500 miles high. It was like another moon, but rather than being round it was square. It was not solid like any other celestial body. It had walls 200 feet thick. This body was built like a gigantic space station where the interior, not the surface, was occupied. That interior, we are told later, was so expansive that a great river flowed through it.

While John stands on that mountain peak watching that unbelievable scene, he observes that this satellite takes a fixed position in the heavens. It hovers in space over the old city of

Jerusalem. Old Jerusalem is less than 15 miles across. This new Jerusalem is 1500 miles in every direction What most impressed John was the brightness of that new body floating in the earth's orbit. It was the same dazzling brightness that John described in chapter four when he stood in heaven before the throne of God. It was the brightness of millions of gems glistening in the sunlight.

So bright was the glow of that heavenly city that there was no need for the sun or moon to give light.He does not say that the sun and moon had been extinguished, but that their light was superfluous. There was no night in that City of God. Nor was there night on earth in the area bathed in its ethereal light.We know that this city did not descend to the earth's surface because John tells us in verse twenty-four that the nations of earth and the kings of the world walked beneath it in its light. This city was big enough to illuminate several nations. If the center of this new Jerusalem centered over old Jerusalem in Palestine, its edges would extend 750 miles in every direction -- reaching to southern Europe, the Ukraine of Russia, parts of China, a large part of Africa and nearly to India. I would have to leave it to NASA scientists to determine at what altitude such a satellite would have to orbit to be stable in space, but more than likely it is several hundred if not thousands of miles above the earth. Of course God could change the rules to bring it a whole lot closer. However close or far it is, the people living on earth have access to go there as often as they wish.

Revelation 21:22-27
Inside the City of God

Would you like to take a glimpse inside that satellite for a preview of what you are going to experience later? Keep in mind that this is not heaven and it is not intended to be our home. We are never going to live in the "New Jerusalem," but we will have access to enter it and leave at will. Our home will be here on earth, but we will be citizens not only of the world, but of the universe. We will have very little need of a particular house to call home. Our physical and social needs will be totally different from what they are now on earth in our mortal bodies. Right now I am a spirit confined to a mortal body. Then I will be a spiritual being with a spiritual body. I will be released from the limitations of mortality and live in a spiritual realm of heavenly beings. We won't be angels, but we will be very similar to them. The difference between us and the angels will be that we will forever maintain a relationship to God as His children. (Rev 21:7)

That relationship is what makes this city of God so special. Jesus the Son had come to earth to live with us as a mortal man. Now God the Father comes to earth and provides mankind with this splendid tabernacle, or meeting place, where we can enjoy the rich glorious fellowship with God. It will be comparable to Adam's meeting with his Creator each day in the cool of the evening.

Although the Bible says that God will dwell in the New Jerusalem, no box 1500 miles square can contain God. He will be there in His fullness but not in His entirety. A pail full of water from the beach is all ocean, but it is not all of the ocean. This satellite city called the throne of God is a place where you and I will be able to bathe in the presence of the eternal omnipotent One we have been taught to call "God the Father." I can understand Jesus and I have come to know Him fairly well. I believe I would feel comfortable if I met Jesus face to face. It has been a little hard for me to get acquainted with God the Father. He is so almighty, so overwhelming, so all consuming, so all knowing, so all encompassing that He has had to stay aloof from mortal human beings.

In the new Jerusalem we will be able to approach God. We won't see Him in bodily form. Yet there will be such warmth, such love, such euphoria, such a sense of well being and such ineffable joy that we will simply want to be there in that Presence. No one will be able to remain in that state of exuberance continually. We will leave and go on with more mundane activities but will always be drawn back to that celestial city to revel in the presence of God Almighty. I have known saints here in this life that I am sure will want to spend most of eternity just being there at the foot of that throne bathed in the shekinah glory of our Heavenly Father. Others of us may visit less often.

There is one last statement that I would like for us to consider in verse 27, which reads:

And there shall in no wise enter into it anything that defileth, neither whatsoever maketh a lie, but they which are written in the Lamb's Book of Life.

This verse implies that there will be inhabitants in the universe who are not believers. The verse could not be referring to human beings because every unbelieving person who had ever lived on earth was cast into the lake of fire following the judgment at the close of chapter twenty. Why is it now that the Word specifically bars any but believers from entering the holy city unless these are beings from another world who could defile it. It is a question to which we do not have a definitive answer, but nevertheless raises a very interesting possibility.

The bright side of the apocalypse. The story recorded by John gets brighter and brighter. It is a glorious revelation that I certainly do not want to miss.

THE BRIGHT SIDE OF THE APOCALYPSE

LESSON XIX

DIVISION SEVEN

Inside the Holy City
Behold I come quickly

Chapter 22

REVELATION CHAPTER TWENTY TWO

The first words of this study were the opening words of the Bible. "...In the beginning." That was the beginning of time. The closing chapter of the Bible deals with the end of time. The thousand years of the millennium have ended. The White Throne judgment has taken place. Eternity has begun. Our existence will be eternal, no longer measured in years. My finite mind cannot comprehend eternity, nor can yours. You and I are headed for eternity. Time, speed and space are so interlinked that it would take another Einstein to be able to calculate what our existence will be like when time shall be no more.

I am sure of one thing. It will be glorious.

This study of the Book of Revelation has centered on the triumph of Christ and of His people, the church. We have seen glimmers of the bright side of the apocalypse. It is evident that God is in control. It is His plan that is being unfolded and not that of Satan. I hope you have seen that plan of redemption in a new light through this study. We have come to the final chapter of that study, a chapter that will give us just a peek at what eternity will be like.

Revelation 22:1-5
]nside the Holy City

The enormous satellite city has settled into a fixed orbit over the ancient city of Jerusalem. We saw what John described as an immense city 1500 miles long, 1500 miles wide and 1500 miles high. Keep in mind that although this satellite is the size of a moon, the city is inside the satellite and not on its surface. I don't have any idea what materials were used in its construction. John tells us its walls were 200 feet thick. From where John stood watching he noted that there were twelve entrances to the city. There were three gates on each of the four walls. You and I will have access to go in and out of any of these gateways.

John is the first to go in. I am sure that he

was overwhelmed at the immensity, the brilliance and beauty of what he saw. There had never been anything like this conceived in the mind of man. The first thing that catches John's eye is a beautiful flowing river. It is not a fountain. It is not a stream. It is a river. Located at the headwaters of that river is the very throne of God. This evidently is no common river. It is the river of life.

John saw streets and trees and amongst those trees on both sides of the river was the tree of life. In Genesis 2:9 we read of the tree of life placed in the garden of Eden for Adam and Eve to eat. After the fall in Genesis 3:22-24 God forbade them to eat of that fruit, but it was not God's intention to keep the fruit of that tree from mankind forever. Jesus promised us in Revelations 3:7 that he that overcomes will eat of the tree of life freely. Now here it is before us in the city of God.

Revelation 22:6-10
Behold I Come Quickly

The Revelation is complete. The book is about to be closed. The end is near. John will finish his life in the first century.He returns to the blistering sands of the Isle of Patmos. It is there on Patmos that the conversation in verse seven takes place. Jesus is talking to John, "BEHOLD I

COME QUICKLY." Some translators say, "I come soon."Quickly is the better rendering. Christ was not coming soon when He spoke those words 2000 years ago -- He was to come in an instant, in the twinkling of an eye.

In verse eight something strange happens. It is curious to me, because this is not the first time it happened. In Revelation 19:10 John experienced the same compulsion to fall before this angel and worship him. The angel who had been John's escort through the Revelation has returned with him to the Isle of Patmos and stands before him. The splendor of this angel overwhelms John. He falls on his face at the angel's feet. Of course the angel recognized that John was doing wrong and forbade him to do it. He then identified himself with these three statements: (1.) I am one of thy fellowservants. (2.) I am one of thy brethren, the prophets (3.) I am one of those overcomers who kept the sayings of this book -- the Bible. This was not an angel. Those statements could only describe a human being. I believe that this "fellow servant" was one of the twelve apostles. I have no idea which one, but probably one of the least known. The word says that the last shall be first and the least shall be the greatest.

EPILOGUE

REVELATION, the unveiling, the revealing. I have seen things revealed in this book that are not disclosed in any other book of the Bible. This may not be the most important book of the holy Scriptures, but it is certainly the most exciting.

Every time I teach this subject and come to the final chapter I sense sadness and regret. I think John must have felt similarly when he was taken back to the hot burning sands of the Isle of Patmos when the Revelation was completed. He had walked the new earth He had seen inside the holy city. He had stood on the brink of eternity. He had been with Jesus and angels and had witnessed spectacular events. Now on the island of Patmos he is revising his notes to give us the final re-write of a book called by the some The Revelation of John. It is hard to come down from those heights. When I teach this book I get caught up in those exciting fantastic scenes depicted by John in his writings. I am sure he was describing events that will soon take place. The events are so real to me that I actually feel drawn into them. I see myself participating in these prophetic scenes and there wells up within me a longing to be there with my Lord. I lament laying the study aside to return to the dismal sin cursed world in which I live.

Don't forget the words of Jesus Christ 'BEHOLD I COME QUICKLY'.

AMEN. EVEN SO, COME, LORD JESUS.